Simone de Beauvoir Today

Conversations 1972–1982

Alice Schwarzer

TRANSLATED FROM THE FRENCH
BY MARIANNE HOWARTH

CHATTO & WINDUS · THE HOGARTH PRESS
LONDON

Published in 1984 by
Chatto & Windus · The Hogarth Press
40 William IV Street
London WC2N 4DF

British Library Cataloguing in Publication Data
Beauvoir, Simone de
  Simone de Beauvoir Today.
  1. Beauvoir, Simone de—Interviews
  I. Title   II. Schwarzer, Alice
  843'.912   PQ2603.E362Z/

ISBN 0 7011 2784 8
ISBN 0 7011 2783 X Pbk

Copyright © 1983 by Rowohlt Verlag GmbH
Copyright in the English translation © 1984 by Marianne
Howarth
Simone de Beauvoir Today was published in Germany in 1983
under the title *Simone de Beauvoir Heute* and in France in 1984
under the title *Simone de Beauvoir: entretiens avec Alice
Schwarzer*.

Printed in Great Britain by
Redwood Burn Ltd
Trowbridge Wiltshire

CONTENTS

Translator's note

These interviews were conducted in French but for the most part first published in translation in various West German journals. Some of them were also published in French journals at the time. All have now been assembled in one volume in each of the two languages. The West German edition is less comprehensive than the French; the French is, therefore, the basis of this English translation. However, where the French version is itself a translation from the German, I have consulted the German text, and I have occasionally – for reasons of clarity – restored material from the German version that had been omitted from the French. The interviews on which this book is based were first published as follows:

'I am a Feminist', *Le Nouvel Observateur*, France, 1972 and *Pardon*, West Germany, 1972; 'We are not above criticism', *Kursbuch*, West Germany, 1973; '*The Second Sex*: thirty years on', *Der Spiegel*, West Germany, 1976 and *Marie-Claire*, France, 1976; 'Women have less far to fall', *Emma*, West Germany, 1978 and *Marie-Claire*, France, 1978; 'A vote against this world', *Emma*, West Germany, 1980; 'Being a woman is not enough', *Der Spiegel*, 1982.

FOREWORD by Simone de Beauvoir

These interviews with Alice Schwarzer took place between the beginning of 1972 and September 1982. Our friendship is both of a personal and a feminist nature, and it has enabled her to put questions of interest to me, and me to respond to them without inhibition. Thus these conversations constitute a very exact account of my attitude to feminism over the period of time during which they took place – an attitude which I still hold today. Indeed, my ideas have scarcely changed since 1970, when I became active in what was then known as the new feminism. However, they have been modified slightly in the light of feminist practice – that is to say, my relationships with other women, the many letters I have received from women, and the various campaigns in which I have taken part. I think it is good for thoughts to be shaped by experience; at any rate, that is the path I have always followed. These interviews should therefore be read in chronological order, as certain modifications were made in the course of time. My attitudes as a feminist are the main topic under discussion. But as Alice Schwarzer had also questioned Sartre and me about our relationship, I considered it appropriate to talk about that in more detail. There are some feminists who do not accept that one may conduct the same struggle as they do, if one is closely linked with one man; I do not agree, and I wanted to explain how it is possible to reconcile the two, at least in my experience. I am glad that this book is being published because it will help my public to know me better and, I hope, to have a better understanding of a cause to which I am deeply attached.

INTRODUCTION

I met her for the first time in 1970. It was not exactly a warm meeting – not on her part anyway. But then, we had met by chance. In fact, I was there because of Sartre. It was during the 'mini-May' in Paris in 1970. For days and weeks, scandalous political trials had been taking place at the State Security Court (a para-military court which was not finally disbanded until after the socialists came to power). Those on trial were mostly French Maoists, the children of May '68, who had been concentrating their work on the factories and shanty towns. At the time, their political role was important as a catalyst for unofficial (and often violent) labour disputes and social protest. Occupying a factory and taking the boss or senior managers hostage had become more or less routine. Government reaction was swift: laws were changed (the maximum sentence for occupying a factory and taking hostages was increased to 'life'), and the police machine was made even more sophisticated. Some of the militant young intellectuals who had gone into the factories and out into the suburbs were arrested or harassed. Others went underground. When the best-known of them went on trial, there were fierce public debates and violent street clashes between demonstrators and the police.

I was working as a foreign correspondent in Paris. My main interests and subject areas were the effects of May 1968, and industrial and social action in particular. One of the burning issues in France and in West Germany at the time was the question of 'revolutionary violence'.

Does one have the right to resist, and if so, how far can 'counter-violence' go?

At the time, Jean-Paul Sartre sympathised openly with the Maoists, serving them both as patron and propagandist; he was legally responsible for the Maoist publication *La Cause du Peuple*, he handed out leaflets outside the Renault factory to demonstrate his support, and made a number of highly-regarded comments on the political trials, the critical tenor of which made the government uneasy. He had agreed to give me an interview on the subject of 'revolutionary violence' on a day when one of these trials was in progress. So there I was in his one-room apartment on the Boulevard Raspail. He had agreed to give me a half-hour interview. As our extremely intense conversation was coming to an end, a key turned in the lock and Simone de Beauvoir came into the room. She gave me a brief irritated look, and then quickly, almost brusquely, reminded Sartre that they had to go to a press conference. Then she sat down at Sartre's desk at the back of the room to wait. She bristled with impatience. I could sense her annoyance at the delay and was embarrassed. It was my first experience of Simone de Beauvoir's 'tête de chameau', her notoriously dismissive manner when situations or people do not suit her. Much later, I realised that she is a very uncompromising person. The other side of the coin is that once she has taken someone to her heart, it takes a lot for her to drop that person.

When the interview was over, the three of us went down in the cramped lift in Sartre's block. She curtly brushed aside my timid attempts at conversation.

It did not matter. For me to come face to face with the author of *The Second Sex* – this 'beacon which Simone de

Beauvoir lit to show women in the second half of this century the way', as a colleague of mine put it a few years ago – was still a truly moving encounter. In the darkness of the Fifties and Sixties, before the new women's movement dawned, *The Second Sex* was like a secret code that we emerging women used to send messages to each other. And Simone de Beauvoir herself, her life and her work, was – and is – a symbol; a symbol of the possibility, despite everything, of living one's life the way one wants to, for oneself, free from conventions and prejudices, even as a woman.

In the months following May 1970, political events came thick and fast. The first women's groups in France were founded that summer. I joined them in September, and the following spring the MLF (Mouvement de la Libération des Femmes) launched a sensational campaign against the ban on abortion. Three hundred and forty-three women, including some very well-known ones, stated publicly that they had had an abortion, and demanded the same right for every woman. Simone de Beauvoir was among them.

Just a few months before, the first French feminist collective publication (*L'an zéro*) had been at great pains to take Simone de Beauvoir to task for being 'Sartre-fixated' and, worse still, for writing for a male publication (*Les Temps Modernes*). Today Simone de Beauvoir still recalls that 'I was very angry about that.'

At the same time, though, some women in the movement did seek contact with her and asked her to join them. And she agreed, quite naturally and without reservation. For us feminists, the fact that she did so was not just a major source of support, it was also a moving gesture of affirmation and encouragement.

In all the years since then, she has never refused anything to the women she worked with politically, or in whom she confided on a personal level. Just as Sartre became a 'compagnon de route' for part of the radical left, so Simone de Beauvoir played the same role for one part of the women's movement, the radical feminists. She gave her support, and indeed still does, to acts of political provocation, took part in various campaigns and contributes her important strategies (for example in 1974, when she proposed a 'League for Women's Rights' – modelled on the 'League for Human Rights' – of which she is still President).

From the end of 1970, I was among the women who worked with her politically. One of the many activities undertaken by the movement was to set up an illegal abortion network and to introduce the new, non-surgical, suction method into France. It was by no means clear at the time whether the Pompidou government would react in a repressive way against the feminists, as it had done against the Maoists, for example. So to cover ourselves, we performed the first abortions in the apartments of so-called 'public figures' (so that if there was a scandal, it would be a real scandal!). Simone de Beauvoir did not hesitate to make her apartment available.

The storm we had unleashed with the abortion campaign, in particular, took us by surprise. The feminist movement had started out with a few dozen activists. By the autumn of 1970, the militants could be numbered in the hundreds in Paris alone. The movement rapidly emerged as a political force in 1970–71, and one to be reckoned with right across the spectrum, from the established parties to alternative groups. Three to four thousand women, Simone de Beauvoir among them, took part in the march for the right to abortion on 11 November 1971.

At the same time, we started organising a 'Tribunal', to be held in February 1972 in the Paris Mutualité. It was to be called 'Days of Denunciation of Crimes against Women'. A handful of women, including Simone de Beauvoir, planned and organised it. Gradually, it became clear that within the MLF, an organisation representing a wide range of issues and political opinion from its inception, Simone de Beauvoir's choice of contacts was by no means haphazard. Then and now, she sought out women who started with a materialist analysis of the situation of women (and the world), and strictly rejected any belief in 'the nature of women'. For example, Anne Zelensky, one of the people who has been active with her in the 'League for Women's Rights'; Christine Delphy, who edits the theoretical feminist publication *(Nouvelles) Questions Feministes*; and the group of women she worked with for many years on 'le sexisme ordinaire' (everyday sexism) for *Les Temps Modernes*.

We all remember the de Beauvoir of those days very well. To begin with, we treated her with a mixture of respect and familiarity, and before long we all became extremely fond of her. She was always on time for our working meetings (unpunctuality is one of her pet aversions), and always got straight down to the matter in hand. Her contributions to discussion were distinguished by a piercing clarity and a devastating disregard for convention (nothing was too radical for her); yet at the same time, her demeanour was sometimes touchingly well brought-up.

The way she could hold her handbag on her lap . . .

It was a period of innovation – everything seemed possible, political work was like a drug filling our entire lives. Evenings of meetings, campaigns, discussions, meals. These meals with de Beauvoir, 'les bouffes', soon became a favourite routine. We took turns cooking the meals (although she never did. She hates cooking!) There were generally six or eight of us, all women. There was much eating, drinking, laughing and making of plans.

It was during one of these 'bouffes' that we came up with the idea for my first interview with Simone de Beauvoir. There were two fundamental reasons behind it. On the one hand, it seemed important to me that the 'conversion' of the author of *The Second Sex* to feminism should be made known to the public – after all, she had always distanced herself from feminism and had often stated her belief that the women's question would be automatically solved within a socialist framework. And on the other, quite simply, we needed the money to hire the Mutualité. The rooms cost 10,000 francs for the weekend; we had raised 8,000, and in fact we came up with the remaining 2,000 by selling the interview to the French weekly, *Le Nouvel Observateur*.

The interview made history. It appeared at the beginning of 1972, at a time when the women's movements in all the Western countries were obstinately insisting on their own identity and so coming into conflict with the left, from which many of the militant activists originally came.

'I am a feminist,' Simone de Beauvoir now declared publicly, and so committed herself to the need for a separate, autonomous women's movement, while also criticising political parties in capitalist and socialist countries alike. The interview was translated into many languages, even Japanese, and a pirated edition did the rounds of several women's groups.

A year later, I made a documentary on Simone de Beauvoir for West German television – in my capacity as a foreign correspondent, I worked mainly for West German radio and television. She enjoyed the filming, despite all the bureaucracy and tedious attention to detail – she is a passionate cinema-goer. The conversation (the second in this book) in which de Beauvoir and Sartre answer questions about their relationship is taken from this broadcast. Conducted in Rome in September 1973, it is, as far as I know, the only interview in which both together answer questions about the ground rules of their relationship – a relationship which has been (and undoubtedly still is) a model for many generations of a partnership joined in love and contracted in freedom.

Those days in Rome marked the beginning of our friendship, over and above our political and journalistic work. I remember particularly the long evenings on the *terrazza*, which de Beauvoir, Sartre and I would spend putting God and the world to rights. One of the things we all three had in common was a love of gossip . . .

It was a brief interlude in our political work, which continued back in Paris. Protest campaigns and feminist activities and initiatives . . . there was nothing we were not ready to take on. Simone de Beauvoir herself always favoured a dual strategy involving both legal and illegal work. However, she never wavered in her rejection of all existing political parties and her decision to work only outside them.

She was, and is, incorruptible. There have been numerous attempts to clip her wings and those of the women's movement, but her reaction has always been one of clear-sighted derision. For example, in our third conversation, held in 1976, her comment on 'International Women's Year' was, 'the next thing will be an International Year of the Sea, then an International Year of the Horse, the Dog, and so on . . . People think of women as objects, that are not worth taking seriously for more than a year in this man's world.'

She constantly reminded us of the central points of her political understanding and analysis, and warned against the new trend, discernible since the mid-1970s, to ascribe a mystic status to motherhood and to believe in the 'nature of women'. 'Given that one can hardly tell women that washing up saucepans is their divine mission, they are told that bringing up children is their divine mission.'

As has so often happened before, her pronouncements, especially those on the subject of motherhood, provoked a storm of protest. Women from all over the world even wrote to her home address in Paris, saying that she was hostile to mothers, that she was frustrated, that she should not throw the baby out with the bathwater. Those who cannot come to terms with the rigour and uncompromising nature of Simone de Beauvoir's thoughts and way of life have always been determined not to understand her.

De Beauvoir has been asked any number of times whether she is not missing something crucial as a non-mother. But has anyone ever asked Sartre whether he feels completely fulfilled as a person, despite the fact that he has never been a father? Because of this inequality, some of her statements on the subject of motherhood understandably reveal a certain irritation, but there is also genuine anger about the way women deceive themselves or are manipulated on this central issue.

What does Simone de Beauvoir say about motherhood? That motherhood is not a woman's life work. That the capacity for biological motherhood (i.e. giving birth) does not automatically mean a duty to be a social mother (i.e. bringing up the child). That motherhood is not in itself a creative act. That in current conditions, motherhood often makes slaves of women and ties them to the house and/or to their role. That we must therefore put an end to this kind of motherhood, and the division of labour along male/female lines. And finally, that the basis of this male/female division of labour is the concept of a 'feminine' maternal nature, invented by men – a maternal nature that is by no means inherent in women, but imposed on them by education. Simone de Beauvoir says, 'Women are exploited – and they allow themselves to be exploited – in the name of love.'* Golden words, now as always.

The re-mystification of motherhood is at the heart of the 'new femininity'. In our third published conversation, held in 1976, we both thought it important to warn against the renaissance of the 'eternal feminine'. Once again, Simone de Beauvoir is sharply critical of any belief that women are 'other', let alone 'superior'. 'That would be the most sinister biological distortion and in total contradiction to everything I think. When men tell us just to go on being a woman, leave all the irksome things, like power, honour, careers to us, be glad that you are as you are, in tune with the earth, preoccupied with human

*This quote has been edited out of the French version. In the German edition it appears in the third interview (Translator's note).

concerns . . . When men say that to us, it is really very dangerous.'

Since then things have gone from bad to worse. Times are getting harder – and the temptation to seek refuge in the fatal illusion of the 'eternal feminine' is ever greater. An international economic crisis and an equally international reassertion of masculinity are both rebounding on us women. The last conversation in this book, held in September 1982, and perhaps the most personal in content and tone, returns in a very topical way to those dangers. It shows Simone de Beauvoir once again as one of the most honest and most radical feminists of our time.

Still the most important theoretician of the new feminism, without whose contribution the new women's movements would certainly not have made as much progress as they have, she relates her observation of the situation today to her personal experience and the tradition she established; she recalls the furore – what a revelation it was – when *The Second Sex* was published in 1949, and shows how the old stereotypes persist.

On the eve of her seventieth birthday, in January 1978, we had a conversation about her own old age. Here, the author of *Old Age* – a work that I believe to be comparable to *The Second Sex* in its radical vision and depth – reveals a trait that I consider very characteristic. Simone de Beauvoir is not a particularly introspective person. The fact that she wrote this comprehensive work on old age does not mean that she has much more to say about her own old age than many other people. In her, this is presumably not just a limitation but also a defence, and it lends her moral strength a touch of ingenuousness.

In her old age Simone de Beauvoir is just the same as she always has been – passionately involved with literature and politics. She still travels a great deal and is surrounded by a small but devoted circle of friends, her 'family'. 'I shall never be alone until the day I die', she says, and she is probably right. Although Sartre, the most important person in her life for over half a century, died in the spring of 1980, she is not at all lonely today.

The shock of Sartre's death is something she has not forgotten; but she has survived it, and reflecting on it has been a great comfort. She overcomes her grief in her latest book, *La Cérémonie des Adieux*, and pays her life companion her final deep respects. With unsentimental accuracy and yet great tenderness, she describes Sartre's last years, and is brave enough to talk about illness and death. She has also published the wonderfully lively and unpretentious conversations about literature that they held during this period, causing another scandal as a result. Is it legitimate to portray such an eminent man in all his frailty and ill-health? Simone de Beauvoir says that one must, because it forms an integral part of his life.

Her modest yet obstinate reserve comes across throughout the book. Whenever Sartre addresses her in the dialogues or wants to talk about her, she interrupts him, 'Don't let's talk about me. This is about you.' But this modesty is backed up by an iron will. Simone de Beauvoir says of herself, 'I have never met anyone, in the whole of my life, who was so well equipped for happiness as I was, or who laboured so stubbornly to achieve it.'

Her happiness was by no means handed to her on a plate; she worked for it enormously hard and with courage. At one point in her memoirs, she describes a stay at an oasis in Algeria. It was 104 °F in the shade. And what was she doing there? 'I was working,' she writes laconically.

But no account of her intelligence and her energy would be complete without mentioning her beauty. Of all the women I know, she is one of the very few – if not the only one – who have fought for the right to be intelligent *and* beautiful, to abound with energy *and* sensuality. One of her former pupils, Sarah Hirschmann, remembers the young teacher in Marseilles: 'She was wearing a lilac silk blouse and a pleated skirt, young, her black hair swept up with combs, in contrast to her light, translucent eyes which were outlined with blue eye-shadow. For years we had been taught by stiff, ageless women with their hair in buns. Miss de Beauvoir seemed unbelievably glamorous.'

Simone de Beauvoir is one of the few women philosophers of modern times, a leading theoretician and a distinguished journalist. She is recognised as a major literary figure both by the critics and by her enormous public who devour her novels and memoirs. It is a record to be proud of. Yet one important aspect is missing from this list: her life, which she has translated into action, over and above her writing and thinking. There, it seems to me, lies the real secret of her fascination and her uniqueness – the interplay and interaction of word and deed. For her, her work is her life.

She is a woman who refuses to accept her role passively, who has taken a stand, flouting all convention and opposition. She never marries – yet her love is deep and faithful. She does not have any children – yet a large part of the younger generation sees her as a model in areas of vital importance. She does not seek to conform – yet she does not evade the issue either; she takes to the battlefield and resists, both physically and intellectually, all pressure, including modish whims. She does not tie herself down, yet she has her roots: in her city, in people and ideas, which she pursues and develops with clarity and consistency, yet she is always ready to change and to radicalise.

She describes and reflects upon her life – in so far as she wants to divulge anything – in her memoirs. Sometimes, though, her novels are actually more revealing. Those which are inspired by her own experience (such as her first book, *She Came to Stay*) seem more powerful to me than those, like *The Blood of Others*, which were written to expound too highly structured an idea. In the last conversation with Sartre, de Beauvoir asks him whether he would prefer to go down in history as a philosopher or a writer, assuming he had to choose. A writer, says Sartre. I put this question indirectly to de Beauvoir and she, too, voted for literature. Comparing her work to Sartre's, she says, 'I set my store by literature.'

If I had to decide, I would ascribe to her more significance as a theorist (without forgetting that her theories only derive their power taken in conjunction with her life and her literary work). *The Second Sex*, her physiological, psychological, economic and historical study of the internal and external reality of women in a male-dominated world, is a pioneering work without parallel. Even today, thirty-three years after it was first published, it is still the most exhaustive and far-reaching theoretical work on the new feminism!

Of course, the new women's movements, which have very complex historical origins and which have emerged all over the Western world, would exist even without Simone de Beauvoir. But I suggest that without her they would still be on very shaky ground today, and that in theoretical terms they would still be labouring with every step across ground which the vanguard has already covered in seven-league boots.

What intellectual freedom, what confidence, what intellectual curiosity and what a lot of hard work it must have taken to produce a work like *The Second Sex*! During the war, women had taken 'men's jobs', and had gained experience and self-confidence. In the years immediately after the war, they were sent back home and they submitted to the dictates of 'femininity' once again. That was when Simone de Beauvoir wrote *The Second Sex*, and raised the banner of revolt. On her own.

Of course, some points in *The Second Sex* are outmoded today (such as her analysis of the historical origins of patriarchy, where the current state of knowledge then resulted in her relying too heavily on Bachofen and Engels). Yet the exhaustive exposition of her own central statement – 'One is not born, but rather becomes, a woman' – is not only as valid today as it has always been, but is even more topical than ever, because of the new mystification of the feminine. Simone de Beauvoir shows us that we can and must shake ourselves out of our slave mentality, though we have been moulded by the dictates of femininity and are trapped by our oppressors, even in our beds. She embodies the existentialist demand that one change from object to subject, refuse to be passive and act in spite of everything, and thus – and at this price – become a human being.

'The majority of women resign themselves to their lot without attempting to take any action; those who have tried to change it have not wanted to be confined by the limits of their peculiarity, so causing it to triumph, but to rise above it. When they have intervened in the course of world affairs, it has been in accord with men, and from a masculine perspective,' de Beauvoir says in *The Second Sex*, and she has been a living example of this all her life. The fate of being a woman has never been a vocation for her. Liberation from this role has always meant breaking out of femininity.

For de Beauvoir the existentialist, 'women's destiny' must be taken as a challenge. Her particular contribution has been to link a profound analysis of the origins of our bonds with the realisation that we women can free ourselves from them, and set out on the uphill path. It is a liberty that has its price.

In the last sentence of *The Second Sex*, Simone de Beauvoir expresses the wish that one day men and women will 'unequivocally affirm their brotherhood'. That is undoubtedly the most daring and most noble vision of a society delivered from the pressure of sex (and other) roles, and from master-slave relationships.

For me, Simone de Beauvoir's life and work represent a challenge for men *and* women alike. Her theories may well provide women with an explanation of their condition, but never an excuse for it.

Alice Schwarzer
Cologne, November 1982

'I am a feminist'

ALICE SCHWARZER] Your analysis of the situation of women is still the most radical we have, in that no author has gone further than you have since your book *The Second Sex* came out in 1949, and you have been the main inspiration for the new women's movements. But it is only now, twenty-three years later, that you have involved yourself actively in women's actual, collective struggle. You joined the International Women's March last November. Why?

SIMONE DE BEAUVOIR] Because I realised that the situation of women in France has not really changed in the last twenty years. There have been a few minor things in the legal sphere, such as marriage and divorce law. And the availability of contraception has increased – but it still does not go far enough, given that only seven per cent of all French women take the Pill. Women haven't made any significant progress in the world of work either. There may be a few more women working now than there were, but not very many. But in any case, women are still confined to the low-grade jobs. They are more often secretaries rather than managing directors, nurses rather than doctors. The more interesting careers are virtually barred to them, and even within individual professions their promotion prospects are very limited. This set me thinking. I thought it was necessary for women who really wanted their situation to change to take matters into their own hands. Also, the women's groups which existed in France before the MLF was founded in 1970 were generally reformist and legalistic. I had no desire to associate myself with them. The new feminism is radical, by contrast. As in 1968, its watchword is: change your life today. Don't gamble on the future, act now, without delay.

When the women in the French women's movement got in touch with me, I wanted to join them in their struggle. They asked me if I would work with them on an abortion manifesto, making public the fact that I, and others, had had an abortion. I thought this was a valid way of drawing attention to a problem which is one of the greatest scandals in France today: the ban on abortion.*

So it was quite natural for me to take to the streets and to join the MLF militants in the march [in November 1971] and to adopt their slogans as my own. Free abortion on demand, free contraception, free motherhood!

A. S.] You refer to the situation in France, yet you have visited several socialist countries. Has the situation of women undergone any fundamental changes there?

S. de B.] It's somewhat different. Almost all Russian women work, and those who do not (the wives of highly placed functionaries and other important men) are held in contempt by the others. Soviet women are very proud of the fact that they work. They have considerable political and social responsibilities and a real sense of these reponsibilities. All the same, if you take into account the number of women in the Central Committee or the People's Assemblies who have any real power, the figure is very low compared with men. The same is true in the professions. The most unappealing and least prestigious jobs are done by women. Almost all doctors in the Soviet Union are women because medical treatment is free, the state does not pay well and the job is extraordinarily hard and tiring.

*A new law was passed in 1975 which permitted abortion in the first ten weeks of pregnancy.

Women are consigned to medicine and education, but the really important jobs, like those in science and engineering, are much less accessible to them. On the one hand, they are not the professional equals of men. On the other, there is the same scandalous situation in Russia as there is everywhere else, which the women's movements are currently fighting – housework and looking after children are exclusively female preserves in the USSR too.

This comes over very strikingly in Solzhenitsyn's *Cancer Ward*. There is a woman in the hospital who is very senior, a very important member of the medical profession; after doing her rounds and after an exhausting day at the hospital, she rushes off home to cook dinner for her husband and children, and to do the washing-up. In other words, she takes on household chores on top of all her heavy professional responsibilities, just as in other countries. Indeed, perhaps even more so than in France where a woman in a similar position would have some domestic help.

The condition of women is, in one sense, better than in the capitalist countries, but it is also more difficult. One concludes that there is no real equality between men and women in the Soviet Union either.

A. S.] Why is that?

S. de B.] First and foremost, because the socialist countries are not really socialist. In other words, they have not achieved the kind of socialism that transforms mankind, which was Marx's dream; what they have done is to change the means of production. But as time goes on, we realise that simply altering the means of production is not sufficient to transform society, to transform people. So despite the different economic system, traditional roles are still allotted to men and women. This is linked with the fact that men in our societies have internalised what I term a superiority complex, an image of their own superiority. They are not prepared to surrender it. They need the inferiority of women to enhance their own status. They need to see women as inferior. And women are so accustomed to think of themselves as inferior that only very rarely do they fight for equality.

A. S.] The term 'feminism' is much misunderstood. What is your definition of it?

S. de B.] At the end of *The Second Sex* I said that I was not a feminist because I believed that the problems of women would resolve themselves automatically in the context of socialist development. By feminist, I meant fighting on specifically feminine issues independently of the class struggle. I still hold the same view today. In my definition, feminists are women – or even men too – who are fighting to change women's condition, in association with the class struggle, but independently of it as well, without making the changes they strive for totally dependent on changing society as a whole. I would say that, in that sense, I am a feminist today, because I realised that we must fight for the situation of women, here and now, before our dreams of socialism come true. Apart from that, I realised that even in socialist countries, equality between men and women has not been achieved. Therefore it is absolutely essential for women to take their destiny into their own hands. That is why I have now joined the Women's Liberation Movement.

There is another reason – and I believe that it is one of the reasons why so many women have come together to found the movement – namely, that a profound inequality exists between men and women even in left-wing and revolutionary groups and organisations in France. Women always do the most lowly, most tedious jobs, all the behind-the-scenes things, and the men are always the spokesmen; they write the articles, do all the interesting things and assume the main responsibility. So, even within these groups, whose theoretical aim is to liberate everybody, including women, even there women are still inferior. It goes still further. Many – not all – men on the left are aggressively hostile to women's liberation. They openly despise us. The first time a feminist meeting took place at Vincennes, a number of male leftists broke into the room shouting, 'Power is at the end of the phallus.' I think they are beginning to revise that position, but only because women are taking militant action independently of them.

A. S.] What is your general position regarding the new feminists, these militant young women who are more radical than ever before?

S. de B.] There is a wide range of tendencies within the women's movements, at least in America, where they have made the most progress. It ranges from Betty Friedan who is fairly conservative to SCUM [the Society for Cutting Up Men] which favours the emasculation of men. And there are any number of positions between the two. In France it seems there are also various tendencies within the movement, and my choice would be one which endeavoured to link women's liberation with the class struggle. I believe that although the women's struggle is unique, it is certainly linked to the struggle women have to conduct along with men. As a result, I reject the total repudiation of men.

A. S.] In that case, what do you think – at the present stage of the conflict – of the exclusion of men from women's meetings, as is the case in most women's movements?

s. de b.] It is, as you have just said, a question of the stage reached. At the moment it's a good thing, for several reasons. First, if men were admitted to these groups, they would not be able to stifle their male reflex to give all the orders and to take charge. On the other hand, many women have a certain feeling – even if they won't admit it – of inferiority, a degree of shyness, and often they know it. Many of them wouldn't dare to speak freely in front of men. It's particularly important for women not to feel judged by the men who share their lives, precisely because they must liberate themselves from them as well . . .

a. s.] . . . and analyse their own specific oppression?

s. de b.] Exactly. At the moment, neither the male mentality, nor the female one, allows a truly honest discussion in a mixed group.

a. s.] Is the exclusion of men at this stage simply a practical question for you, because women would be more inhibited or whatever? Or is it also a political question? Given that men represent the system, and, furthermore, that men as individuals oppress women, are they not therefore seen as Enemy Number One in the initial stages?

s. de b.] Yes, of course, but it is fairly complicated, because what Marx says about capitalists applies here. They are victims too. Of course, it is too abstract to say, as I did for a time, that one must only fight the system. Of course one must fight men as well. After all, one is an accomplice, one still profits by the system, even if one hasn't created it oneself. The man of today didn't set up this patriarchal society but he profits from it, even if he is one of those who are critical of it. And he has made it very much a part of his own unconscious thinking.

One must fight the system, but at the same time one must approach men, if not with hostility exactly, then at least with suspicion, and with caution, and not let them trespass on our activities, our own potentialities. Women must attack both the system and men. Even if a man is a feminist, one should still keep one's distance and be wary of paternalism. Women don't want to be granted equality; they want to win it, which is not the same thing at all.

A. S.] Have you ever felt this suspicion, this hatred of men?

s. de B.] No. I have always got on very well with the men in my life. Indeed, many of the women I know in the MLF don't hate men either, but they do take a cautious attitude, and are determined not to let men devour them.

A. S.] Do you think that it's a good thing, politically, for some women to go further than that?

s. de B.] Perhaps. Perhaps it's not a bad thing that some women are really totally, totally radical and repudiate men completely. These women might be able to win over those who out of a lack of personal motivation might otherwise be ready to compromise. That's entirely possible.

A. S.] In most women's movements there is a homosexual element – by no means the majority, incidentally, as is so often said, but a minority – which is a source of important ideas nonetheless. Do you believe that female homosexuality – the most radical way of excluding men – can be a political weapon in the current phase?

s. de B.] I haven't thought about that. I think it's a very good thing that some women are very radical. Lesbians could play a useful part. But when they put too much emphasis on their homosexuality, they risk alienating the heterosexuals from the movement. I find their mystique of the clitoris fatuous and irritating, as well as the sexual dogmas they try to impose.

A. S.] These homosexual women have taken it upon themselves to refrain from all sexual relations with men because under current conditions they must necessarily be oppressive . . .

S. de B.] Is it true that all sexual relations between a man and a woman are necessarily oppressive? Instead of refusing such relations, could one not work at them so that they are not oppressive? I'm shocked when people tell me that intercourse is always rape. I don't believe it. When one says that intercourse is rape, basically one is adopting male myths. That would mean that the male sex organ really is a sword, a weapon. It's a question of inventing new, non-oppressive sexual relations.

A. S.] You said in a comment on *The Second Sex* that the problem of femininity had never affected you personally, that you found yourself 'in a position of great impartiality'. Do you mean to say that individually a woman can escape her female condition? Professionally, as well as in her relationships with her fellow human beings?

S. de B.] Escape one's female condition completely? No! I have the body of a woman – but clearly I have been very lucky. I have escaped many of the things that enslave a woman, such as motherhood and the duties of a housewife. And professionally as well – in my day there were fewer women who studied than nowadays. And, as the holder of a higher degree in philosophy, I was in a privileged position among women. In short, I made men recognise me: they were prepared to acknowledge in a friendly way a woman who had done as well as they had, because it was so exceptional. Now that many women undertake serious study, men are fearful for their jobs. Admitting, as I have done, that a woman doesn't necessarily have to be a wife and mother to have a fulfilled and happy life, means that there will be a certain number of women who will be able to have fulfilled lives without suffering the enslavement of women. Of course they have to be born into a privileged family or possess certain intellectual abilities.

A. S.] You once said, 'the greatest success of my life is my relationship with Sartre' . . .

S. de B.] Yes.

A. S.] . . . yet all your life you have always had a great need for your own independence and a fear of being dominated. Given that it is very difficult to establish relationships between men and women that are based on equality, do you believe that you personally have succeeded?

S. de B.] Yes. Or rather, the problem never arose, because there is nothing of the oppressor about Sartre. If I'd loved someone other than Sartre, I would never have let myself be oppressed. There are some women who escape male domination, mostly by means of their professional autonomy. Some have a balanced relationship with a man. Others have inconsequential affairs.

A. S.] You have described women as an inferior class . . .

S. de B.] I didn't say class. But in The Second Sex I did say that women were an 'inferior caste', a caste being a group one is born into and cannot move out of. In principle, though, one can transfer from one class to another. If you are a woman, you can never become a man. Thus women are genuinely a caste. And the way women are treated in economic, social and political terms makes them into an inferior caste.

A. S.] Some women's movements define women as a class outside the existing classes. They base this on the fact that housework, which has no exchange value, is done exclusively by women for nothing. As they see it, patriarchal oppression is therefore the main contradiction, not a subsidiary one. Do you agree with this analysis?

S. de B.] I find the analysis lacking on this point. I'd like someone to do some serious work on it. In *Women's Estate*, for example, Juliet Mitchell showed how to ask the question, but she doesn't claim to resolve it in that book. I remember it was one of the first questions I put when I first came into contact with the militant feminists in the MLF: what, in your view, is the exact connection between patriarchal oppression and capitalist oppression? At the moment, I still don't know the answer. It's a problem which I'd very much like to work on in the next few years. I'm extremely interested in it. But the analyses which regard patriarchal oppression as the equivalent of capitalist oppression are not correct in my view. Of course, housework doesn't produce any surplus value. It's a different condition to that of the worker who is robbed of the surplus value of his work. I'd like to know exactly what the relationship is between the two. Women's entire future strategy depends upon it.

It's very right to emphasise unpaid housework. But there are many women who earn their own living, and who cannot be considered as exploited in the same way as housewives are.

A. S.] But even when a woman does work outside the house, she is paid less than a man for the same job.

s. de b.] Yes, wages are not the same. That's true. But to return to my point. The exploitation of women doing housework is not the same thing as worker exploitation. This is a point that neither Kate Millet nor Germaine Greer nor Shulamith Firestone pays enough attention to.

a. s.] They bring nothing new to the analysis . . .

s. de b.] No. Not in the case of Millet or Greer. But Firestone, who is less well-known, does include something new in her book *The Dialectic of Sex*. She links women's liberation with children's liberation. That is correct, because women will not be liberated until they have been liberated from their children, and by the same token, until children have also been liberated from their parents.

a. s.] You've also been very active in the class struggle, since May 1968. For instance, you've assumed responsibility for a radical left magazine. You've taken to the streets. In brief, what is the connection between the class struggle and the war between the sexes, in your opinion?

s. de b.] What I have been able to establish is that the class struggle in the strict sense does not emancipate women. That has made me change my mind since *The Second Sex* was published. It doesn't matter whether you're dealing with Communists, Trotskyists or Maoists, women are always subordinate to men. As a result, I'm convinced of the need for women to be truly feminist, to take their problems into their own hands. A serious analysis is needed to try to establish the relationship between worker exploitation and the exploitation of women, and to what extent the overthrow of capitalism would create better conditions for the emancipation of women. I don't know. It still remains to be done. I'm certain of one thing though, which is that the overthrow of capitalism would create more favourable conditions for the emancipation of women at a stroke. But there would still be a long way to go to achieve it.

Overthrowing capitalism does not mean overturning the patriarchal tradition so long as the family is left intact. I believe that one must not only overthrow capitalism and transform the means of production, but that one must also change the structure of the family. And that has not been done, not even in China. Of course, the feudal family has been abolished, and by the same token a change in the position of women has been achieved. But in the sense that they accept the nuclear family, which is, in fact, the successor to the feudal family, I really don't believe that women in China are liberated. I think that the family must be abolished. I'm in complete agreement with the attempts made by women, and indeed sometimes by men too, to replace the family either with communes or with other forms which have yet to be invented.

A. S.] So could one say that the class struggle doesn't necessarily change women's condition, but conversely that radical feminism – calling society and the relations between men and women into question – will destroy the classes?

S. de B.] No, not necessarily. If you start by destroying the family and related structures, then there's a possibility that capitalism will start to teeter at the same time. But I don't want to go too far along those lines either, without having thought about it properly. I don't know to what extent the destruction of patriarchal society by women would affect all aspects of capitalism and democracy.

If feminism makes radical demands and if it manages to implement them, then it really will be a threat to the system. But that will not be enough to reorganise the means of production or the conditions of work or the relationships of men – by which I mean human beings – to one another. There hasn't been enough analysis of this point; and that is because the women who have been active in feminism have mostly been middle-class women who conducted their struggle within the political system.

I'm thinking of the suffragettes, who sought the right to vote. They were not thinking of themselves in economic terms. And, in economic terms, we have tended to settle for Marxist formulas and to assume that socialism, when it came, would mean equality between men and women at a stroke. When I wrote *The Second Sex*, I was very surprised at the bad reception it got from the left. I remember one discussion I had with the Trotskyists who said that the women's problem was not a true problem, and that it simply didn't exist. When the revolution came, women would automatically find their place.

It was the same with the Communists, with whom I was in very bad political odour at the time, and who exposed me to a great deal of ridicule. They wrote articles saying that the working-class women in Billancourt really couldn't give a damn about the women's problem. Once the revolution had taken place, women would be equal with men. But they were not interested in what would happen to women in the time it took for the revolution to come.

I also hoped that things would be a great deal better in the socialist countries than in the capitalist ones. Well, that hope was pretty smartly dashed – apart from the few shades of difference that I referred to earlier.

A. S.] After *The Second Sex* was published, you were

often accused of not having developed any tactics for the liberation of women and of having come to a halt in your analysis.

s. de b.] That's right. I admit it was a shortcoming in my book. I finish with vague confidence in the future, the revolution and socialism.

a. s.] And today?

s. de b.] I have changed my views now. As I've been telling you, I really am a feminist.

a. s.] What concrete possibilities do you see for the liberation of women on an individual and on a collective level?

s. de b.] On an individual level, women must work outside the home. And, if possible, they should refuse to get married. I could have married Sartre but I think we were wise not to have done so, because when you are married, people treat you as married and eventually you think of yourself as married. As a married woman, you simply do not have the same relationship with society as an unmarried woman. I believe that marriage is dangerous for a woman.

Having said that, there can be reasons for it – if you want to have children, for example. Having children is still very difficult if the parents are not married because the children encounter all sorts of difficulties in life.

What really counts, if one wants to be truly independent, is work, a job. That is my advice to all women who ask me. It is a necessary precondition. If you are married and want a divorce, it means you can leave, and support your children, and have a life of your own. Of course, work is not a miracle cure. Work today does have a liberating side, but it is also alienating. As a result, many women have to choose between two sorts of alienation:

the alienation of the housewife and that of the working woman. Work is not a panacea, but all the same, it is the first condition for independence.

A. S.] And what about the women who are already married and have children?

S. de B.] I think there are some women who really don't stand much of a chance. If they are thirty-five, with four children to cope with, married and lacking any professional qualfications – then I don't know what they can do to liberate themselves. You can only talk about the real prospect of liberation for future generations.*

A. S.] Can women who are struggling for their liberation do so as individuals, or must they act collectively?

S. de B.] They must act collectively. I myself have not done so up to now because there was no organised movement with which I was in agreement. But all the same, writing *The Second Sex* was an act which went beyond my own liberation. I wrote that book out of concern for the feminine condition as a whole, not just to reach a better understanding of the situation of women, but also to contribute to the struggle and to help other women to understand themselves.

In the last twenty years I have received an enormous number of letters from women telling me that my book has been a great help to them in understanding their situation, in their struggle and in making decisions for themselves. I've always taken the trouble to reply to these women. I've met some of them. I've always tried to help women in difficulties.

A. S.] What is your general opinion of the way the existing women's movements have developed?

*Note on French text in Simone de Beauvoir's handwriting: 'See third interview for criticism of that idea' (Translator's note).

s. de B.] I think they'll make progress. But I'm not sure. In France, like everywhere else, most women are very conservative: they want to be 'feminine'. All the same, I think that the modern conditions of housework are liberating women a little and giving them a little more time to reflect: they must be led into revolt. In professional terms, there is no doubt that women will never get work in a capitalist country while men are unemployed. That's why I think women will never achieve equality unless there is a complete overthrow of the system.

I think the women's movement could have the same effect as the student movements, which were also limited to begin with, but later set off a wave of strikes throughout the country; it could cause an explosion. If women get a foothold in the world of work, they could really shake up the system. At the moment, though, the weakness of the French movement, and of the American movement too, I believe, is that there are so few working-class women in it.

A. S.] Isn't it a case of the stage reached in the struggle?

s. de B.] Of course. Everything is connected. When women go on strike, as they did in Troyes and Nantes, they become aware of their power and their autonomy, and they are much less ready to submit at home.

A. S.] So you think there is a need to develop this sense of solidarity?

s. de B.] Absolutely. Liberation on an individual level is not enough. There must be a collective struggle, at the level of the class struggle too. Women fighting for women's liberation cannot be truly feminist without being part of the left, because even though socialism is not sufficient to guarantee the equality of the sexes, it is still necessary.

A. S.] Indeed, for the first time in history feminist movements are also revolutionary movements. They don't believe there can be any changes in the lot of women without changes to society as a whole.

S. de B.] True. There was a slogan I saw in Italy which I found very apt: 'No revolution without women's liberation, no liberation of women without revolution.'

A. S.] In *The Second Sex* you quoted Rimbaud's vision of a future world in which women would be liberated. Do you have a vision of this new world?

S. de B.] Rimbaud was imagining that women would contribute something entirely different to the world after their liberation. I don't believe that. I don't think that, having achieved equality, women will develop any specifically feminine values. I've discussed this with some Italian feminists. They say we must reject masculine values and models, we should invent some that are entirely different. I don't agree. The fact is that culture, civilisation and universal values have all been created by men, because men represented universality. But just as the proletariat rejects the notion that the bourgeoisie is the universal class, though without rejecting the entire bourgeois heritage, so women should make use of some of the tools men have created, from a position of equality with men. I think that a degree of suspicion and vigilance is necessary here too.

In creating universal values – by which I mean mathematics, for example – men have often left their specifically masculine, male, virile stamp on them. They have combined the two in a very subtle and devious way. So it's a question of separating one from the other and of getting rid of this confusion. It is possible, and that is one of the tasks women face. When it comes down to it, what do we mean by rejecting the male model? If a woman learns karate, it is a masculine thing. We ought not to reject the world of men, because, after all, it is our world too.

I believe that liberated women will be just as creative as men. But I do not think women will create new values. If you believe the opposite, then what you are believing in is a feminine nature – which I have always opposed. We must totally reject all concepts of that kind.

Of course, women's liberation will lead to new kinds of relationships between human beings and men and women will certainly be changed. Women, and men too, must become total human beings. The differences between them are no more important than the differences between men and women on an individual level.

A. S.] Do you believe in the need for violent tactics in bringing about the liberation of women?

S. de B.] In the present situation, yes – up to a point. Because men resort to violence against women – in their use of language, in gesture. They rape them, insult them, even the way they look at them can be aggressive. Women should use violence to defend themselves. Some women are learning karate or other forms of self-defence. I'm entirely in favour of that. They'll feel much more at ease in themselves and in the world if they don't feel helpless in the face of male aggression.

A. S.] You often talk about American women. Has your main contact with feminism been through them?

S. de B.] Yes; primarily through their books. There are many of them, apart from those we've already mentioned, Kate Millet and Germaine Greer – although they are not American – and Shulamith Firestone. I've read their books. So far French women have not published anything. It has to be said that the American women's movement is more advanced. I've also had a lot of letters from American women and invitations to visit America. But my reply to them is that I'm working with French women, and that I must work at home first.

A. S.] Now that you describe yourself as a militant feminist and have involved yourself in the active debate, what action to you intend to take in the immediate future?

S. de B.] I'm working on a project with a group of women. We want to organise a kind of public hearing to denounce the crimes committed against women. The first two days will be devoted to questions of motherhood, abortion and contraception, and will take place on 13 and 14 May in the Mutualité hall in Paris. There will be a sort of committee of enquiry composed of about ten women. They will cross-examine the witnesses, who will include biologists, sociologists, psychiatrists, doctors, midwives and, above all, women who have suffered from the conditions society imposes upon women.

We hope to convince the public that women must be assured of the right to procreate freely, of public support for the burdens of motherhood – especially crèches – and of the right to refuse unwanted pregnancies through contraceptive measures and abortion. We are demanding that these be free and that women have the right to choose.

A. S.] The struggle of the women's liberation movements is often linked with the struggle for free abortion. Do you personally want to go beyond this stage?

S. de B.] Of course. I think the women's movements, including me, will have to work together on many things. We are not only fighting for free abortion but also for widespread availability of contraceptives, which will mean that abortion will only play a marginal role. On the other hand, contraception and abortion are only a point of departure for the liberation of women. Later on, we will be organising other meetings at which we will expose the exploitation of female labour, be it as a housewife, a white-collar worker, or a working-class woman.

Paris, 1972

'We are not above criticism'

SIMONE DE BEAUVOIR & JEAN-PAUL SARTRE
talking about their relationship.

ALICE SCHWARZER] Simone, you wrote: 'My most important work is my life,' and 'the most outstanding experience of my life was meeting Sartre.' That was forty years ago and you have been together ever since; but at the same time you have tried to escape from possessiveness, jealousy, fidelity and monogamy. You have been criticised by many people for your way of life; many people have tried to imitate you. Deliberately or not, you have become something of an ideal, a model for many couples; and especially for many women, who have been guided by your theories, your practice and your life. In this context, I'd like to ask you some questions about your relationship. First, whether the fact that you have never lived together was not actually more important than the fact that you have never married?

SIMONE DE BEAUVOIR] Undoubtedly! Because when a so-called free relationship is run on the same lines as a marriage – if you have a joint household and eat together regularly – the woman will play her traditional feminine role in spite of everything. And that is only marginally different from being married. We, on the other hand, have a very flexible way of life which has sometimes allowed us to live under the same roof without living together completely. For example, when we were quite young, we lived in hotels, ate in restaurants, sometimes together, sometimes with friends. We went on holidays together, but then not always and not for the whole time. For example, I enjoy walking, Sartre doesn't, so I would set off on my own and he would spend the time with friends. This kind of freedom, which we have maintained in our everyday lives, is important, and it has prevented a sterile daily routine from insinuating itself between us. I think that was more important than the fact that we

never went through a formal ceremony of marriage.
A. S.] You decided not to live together. Perhaps this kind
of thing is easier if you have material advantages?
JEAN-PAUL SARTRE] Yes, I think so.
S. de B.] We were not very well off, but we both had a
teacher's salary, and so we could each afford a small
hotel room. But if you don't earn very much, it's very
difficult to run to that kind of expense. The idea of not
living together came about because neither of us wanted
to saddle ourselves with a house. We lived in hotels. I
couldn't ever imagine having an apartment. At the time,
it was not just that we didn't want to settle down together
but that we didn't want to settle down at all, so to speak.
A. S.] But there was a time when you lived together in
the same hotel, wasn't there?
J.-P. S.] Oh yes.
S. de B.] Oh yes. Quite often, in fact. We almost always
lived in the same hotel, sometimes on different floors,
sometimes on the same floor. But it still meant a great
deal of independence.
A. S.] After reading your memoirs, I wonder whether
you really wanted to call monogamy into question, or
rather whether you both attached absolute priority to
your mutual relationship, and so relegated all third
parties to a secondary role?
S. de B.] That's it exactly.
J.-P. S.] Yes, there is something in what you say. That
was what brought me into conflict with other women.
Because they always wanted the main role.
S. de B.] That is, third parties, in Sartre's life as well as in
mine, always knew from the start about our relationship
and that it would put pressure on any relationship either
of us had with them. They didn't always like it very much

– in fact they were sometimes very hurt. So our relationship is not above criticism, any more than anyone else's, because it has sometimes meant that we didn't behave very well towards other people.

A. S.] So other people have suffered?

S. de B.] Yes, exactly.

A. S.] And the decision – assuming there was one – not to have children: or was that something neither of you ever felt the need to discuss?

S. de B.] For me it went without saying. Not because I would have loathed the idea of bringing up children *per se*. When I was still very young and was thinking about a bourgeois marriage to my cousin Jacques, that would have meant children. But my relationship with Sartre was such – it was, above all, on an intellectual rather than an institutional or familial basis – that I never had any desire for children. I had no special wish to have a reproduction of Sartre – he was enough for me! – and no wish to have a reproduction of myself either: I was enough for me. I don't know – did the question arise with you, Sartre?

J.-P. S.] I didn't think about having children when I was young.

A. S.] But you've adopted a daughter now?

J.-P. S.] That's very different. It's a freely-chosen relationship. She's not so much a daughter . . . I adopted her more to do her, and me, a favour.

S. de B.] It was more that it was a great joy for her to have some kind of paternal relationship. She had not been very happy in her family. She wanted to have another father. But, more importantly, she is someone who has been chosen, chosen as an adult . . . how old was she when you adopted her?

J.-P. S.] Twenty-six or twenty-eight.

A. S.] And it's not a bit like being a substitute father for you?

J.-P. S.] No, it's more like being a social father, if you like, because it gives me certain rights which have made her life easier. It was not really a family matter for me.

S. de B.] There was also a purely practical aspect: Sartre very much wanted to have someone who could legally inherit, not so much the money, which is not important, but the rights to his work, because it is very unpleasant to know that your intellectual estate is in the hands of distant cousins or people who have certain powers over it without having the least affinity with you. So somebody who had been especially chosen, who was much younger and was therefore very likely to outlive him seemed a practical precaution.

A. S.] To return to your decision not to have any children: it's often said, of women especially, that they will regret decisions like that later, when it's too late. Has that happened to you, Simone?

S. de B.] Not at all! I have never regretted not having children, because I've had a lot of good luck, not only in my relationship with Sartre but with my friends too. In fact, when I consider the relationships the women I know have with their children, especially with their daughters, they often seem dreadful to me. I am genuinely glad to have escaped that.

A. S.] What are your ground rules as a couple? Do you always tell each other the truth, for example?

J.-P. S.] I feel I have always told the truth, but that I've done so spontaneously. It wasn't necessary to ask me questions. One doesn't always tell the truth straight away – maybe a week or a fortnight later. But one does tell the truth, the whole truth, always. At least I do! And she . . .

s. de b.] I do, I do. But I don't think you can raise our example to the level of a general rule. Honesty suited us. And then, we are intellectuals and know very well – as Sartre has said – whether one has to tell the truth today or a week later, whether one has to be tactical, etc . . . But one cannot advise all couples to be brutally frank with one another all the time. On occasions, there's even a way of using the truth as a weapon of aggression – men often do that. They're not only unfaithful to their wives, but they actually enjoy telling them about it, more for their own personal satisfaction than for any reasons of honesty in their relationship with the other person. I wouldn't elevate the truth to the status of a value in itself. It is a joy to be able to tell each other everything, but not a value in itself.

a. s.] Many people regard you as 'Sartre's companion'. But Sartre has never been 'de Beauvoir's companion'. Has this distinction had an effect on your relationship? Has it ever annoyed you or upset you or put a strain on you?

s. de b.] It has had absolutely no effect on my relationship with Sartre because after all, it was not his fault. And it didn't bother me all that much either, because I had a certain amount of personal recognition through my writing, as well as being very close to certain women and to some of my readers.

Of course, it did annoy me sometimes to read reviews saying I probably would never have written a single line if I hadn't met Sartre, or that Sartre made my literary career, or even – as some have claimed – that Sartre wrote my books.

a. s.] Sartre, how did you react to smears like that?

j.-p. s.] I thought they were utterly ridiculous. I never

protested because they were only rumours, and not articles worth taking seriously. It didn't bother me personally, not because I am a man who is so confident of his own masculinity, but because they were totally insignificant, because it was just tittle-tattle. It was never a threat or a cause of concern to our relationship.

A. S.] I'd like to ask you a banal question, but one which seems important to me nonetheless, about the practical side of your relationship. Money often plays a large part between couples; material questions are very important. Has money ever been an issue between you?

J.-P. S.] Not between us. Of course, money has been important for each of us, for both of us, and on occasions for both of us together, because one has to live. But it has never been a problem between us, it has never affected our relationship. Either we both had money, or the one who had some shared it. Either we shared it, or we lived separately, all depending.

S. de B.] When we were young, Sartre had a tiny legacy from his grandmother, and I never had any scruples about his using it so that we could travel together. We never had any particularly strong rules. There were times when I was literally living on Sartre's money because I wanted to write – *The Second Sex*, I think it was. If I'd taken a job I wouldn't have been able to write. And he had quite a lot of money at the time. It didn't worry me. A couple of years ago, things weren't going too well for him, and I helped him out. So there are no problems, one person's money is the other person's too, even though our funds are separate and we don't have to account for them. I do what I want with my money and he does the same with his. But, in a sense, it's the same.

A. S.] So if I understand you correctly, you were

financially dependent on Sartre while you were writing *The Second Sex*?

s. de b.] I don't remember exactly if it was *The Second Sex*, but this is what happened. It was after the war and I had left teaching. I could have returned to it – I had been officially reinstated – but I had absolutely no desire to teach while I had books to write and while Sartre had a lot of money and was kind enough to lend me some. We shared everything as we always had done, except that at the time he was quite well off and I wasn't. It really didn't bother me, because if I had wanted to, if I had fallen out with him or whatever, I could have always found another teaching post. I retained my independence, in essence. I regarded it as a favour from a friend and one which I would do for a friend – male or female – and which, incidentally, Sartre has also done for other people he has close ties with.

a. s.] When you have as close a relationship as you do, you have an influence on each other. Can you, Sartre, or you, Simone, say on what points you have influenced one another?

j.-p. s.] I would say that we have influenced each other totally.

s. de b.] On the contrary, I think that it is not influence but a kind of osmosis.

j.-p. s.] If you like. On particular questions – not only literary ones but matters of our lives as well – we always reach a joint decision and each of us influences the other.

s. de b.] Yes, that is exactly what I mean by osmosis. We reach our decisions jointly and we almost develop our thoughts jointly. So there are points on which Sartre has influenced me. For instance, he is primarily a philosopher and I have adopted his philosophical ideas. Other things came from me, particular ways of living for example, or the way we travel, where I nearly always had things my way; especially when we had no money, which made travelling rather difficult. Sartre enjoyed travelling but he wouldn't have made all the sacrifices I demanded of him – sleeping out of doors, walking . . .

A. S.] How did you generally react to that? Did you protest, Sartre?

J.-P. S.] No, I did what had to be done.

S. de B.] Oh, he had his own special way of registering a protest. He had his pills, or he had his tired phases . . . But generally he did do what had to be done . . . And there was another thing as well, not exactly an influence, namely the fact that we always show each other everything we write. Sartre has criticised everything I have written, and I have criticised almost everything he has written. And sometimes we don't have exactly the same opinion. With some books he has said to me, I don't think you will finish that, leave it be . . . But I stuck to my guns. And when I was still very young, I said to him, I think you ought to devote yourself to literature rather than philosophy – but he still stuck to his guns. Fortunately! Each of us is independent within our life together.

A. S.] I am rather astonished to hear you using the polite form 'vous' to one another. Five years after the events of May 1968, you are both more or less committed to revolutionary movements where it is customary to use the familiar 'tu'. Why do you use the polite form to each other, and what importance do you attach to it now, Sartre?

J.-P. S.] Well, I didn't start it. Simone de Beauvoir addresses me in the polite form. I accepted it and now I'm quite used to it. I couldn't use the familiar form with her now.

s. de B.] Well, I've always found it very difficult to address people in the familiar, I don't know why, though I did so with my parents and that should have enabled me to do so with other people too. My best friend Zaza always addressed her girl friends in the familiar, but she used the polite form with me because I did so with her. And now I address my best friend Sylvie in the polite form, in fact I address nearly everybody in the polite form, apart from one or two people who have forced the familiar on me. And I say 'vous' to Sartre. This has been a habit with me for many years, so of course we don't want to play the 1968 revolutionary all of a sudden and start saying 'tu' . . .

A. s.] Do you believe now, given your long experience, that you have escaped the traditional relationship between man and woman, and the roles associated with it as much as possible – if not completely?

s. de B.] I don't think that, given the way of life we have chosen, I have often had to play the female role. Only once, as I remember: it was during the war when somebody had to attend to things like groceries and travel arrangements and do a bit of cooking. And of course I did, not Sartre. He was completely incapable of doing so because he is a man. Though I have had a lot of contact with other men who were different. I'm thinking of one of our very good friends who had been brought up completely differently; he had been a boy scout or something and often did his own housework. During the war, we often went out to the suburbs of Paris for meat, we often peeled the beans together. I don't think it was because of my relationship with Sartre that I took on these domestic chores – it was much more because Sartre couldn't do them himself. But that is only the result of his masculine upbringing which kept him at one remove from various household chores. I think the only thing he can do is fried eggs.

J.-P. S.] Yes, something like that.

A. S.] Women who would have liked to have known that there was at least one emancipated woman have sometimes been disappointed by some of the things in your memoirs . . . For example, when you were talking about your relationship with Olga, you said 'I was annoyed' or 'irritated' or something similar, 'but Sartre liked her a great deal and so I made an effort to see things his way, because it was very important to me to agree with Sartre on all matters.' And I remember another incident when you, Jean-Paul Sartre, came back from the war and said, 'Simone, we shall go into politics now,' and you write, 'so we went into politics.'

S. de B.] I don't think I reacted like that because I am a woman. You see, many of our male friends, who were very confused and didn't know what to do, had the same reaction and were in favour of political work. That is one of Sartre's qualities, in fact. He creates possibilities: sometimes they turn out not to be viable, but he opens up these pathways all the same. At the time, it was not just me; almost all our younger friends and even those of our age took their cue from him. He had a certain authority as someone who had been interned. So it was not so much a question of the relationship between a man and a woman. As to the first point you mentioned: I have always needed to be in agreement with Sartre on all points, on important things, yes, that has always been essential for me. I don't know whether you . . .

J.-P. S.] For me too, absolutely.

S. de B.] I don't think you would have accepted a great distance between us.

A. S.] Could you have said the same thing?

J.-P. S.] Yes, certainly.

A. S.] Simone, you have been associated with the women's movement for two years now. I would like to take this opportunity of asking Sartre a question: what do you think of the autonomous women's liberation struggle?

J.-P. S.] What do you mean by 'autonomous'?

A. S.] The political struggle of women's organisations or groups, independent of men.

J.-P. S.] As far as the relationship between men and women is concerned, I am in complete agreement with Simone de Beauvoir. But I have often wondered whether it is necessary to exclude men from feminist organisations. I cannot really say at this stage, because I do appreciate that it is necessary for women at the moment. Yet I wonder whether it is the correct form of struggle. Might it not be important to include men who think the same way?

S. de B.] But men never think exactly the same way as women!

J.-P. S.] So you keep telling me.

S. de B.] Yes, exactly.

J.-P. S.] It would be better if you acknowledged that you don't trust me on this point.

S. de B.] Even you, theoretically and ideologically a supporter of the liberation of women through and through, all the same, even you do not share everything that women – including me – term their women's experience. There are some things you cannot understand. Sylvie – who is also very close to the MLF – and I often attack you on that point. For example, Alice was saying recently that she cannot go out for a walk on the streets of Rome without feeling harassed all the time – that is simply not within your experience as a man. And when I told you about it, you said, 'What you say doesn't affect me particularly because I have never behaved in an aggressive way towards women.'

A. S.] That is more a reactionary response really. Would you also say, 'The fact that classes exist is not a bad thing because I, Sartre, have never done a worker any harm?' You would never dare!

J.-P. S.] But that isn't the same thing at all.

S. de B.] All the same, it is not so far removed. However well-disposed they might be, men have a lot of trouble understanding the aggression women suffer. Especially those of Sartre's generation. But I do know some younger ones – around thirty-five or so – who are very sensitive to it, at least where the women of their generation are concerned. But I think there is another thing: when I was young, I was never so exposed to aggression of this kind. Men have obviously changed. I think that the emancipation of women has actually made them more hostile towards women than they were; they have become more aggressive, more pushy, more sarcastic and more offensive, than they were in my time.

A. S.] Sartre, you said that you agree theoretically with Simone de Beauvoir on the women's question. So you would admit that there is specific oppression of women, exercised both by the system as a whole and by men individually. And if I'm not mistaken, in your political theory and practice, the oppressed generally tend to have right on their side. In other words, you would never take the liberty of telling a worker what action to take or how to organise himself. How is it that you don't take the same attitude where women are concerned?

J.-P. S.] First, I must say that Castor* is exaggerating when she says that I have absolutely no experience of what it is like to be humiliated as a woman just because I am a man. Whenever women of my acquaintance tell me that they have been victims of such persecution in the course of the day, it always affects me – I am appalled! So although I cannot experience exactly the same thing as they do, I do have the experience of a person who sees people he loves being the object of very unpleasant treatment. That is all I can say on that. But what was your question exactly?

A. S.] For the last five years there have been women's groups in America and other Western countries – and in France too – who see themselves as participants in revolutionary movements and whose experience leads them to the conclusion that women are intimidated in the presence of men, even when men are well-disposed towards them (and such men do exist). There are very subtle power structures which women simply cannot liberate themselves from in the presence of men! That's why, to go back to what I said before, I am surprised that you, Sartre, have no view, no really clear answer to this demand, to the right women have to political autonomy – at the present stage of the struggle, not as an objective in itself, of course.

J.-P. S.] Well, to begin with, I do indeed believe that women are oppressed, and that men go to great lengths to treat them as the 'second sex', in the sense of Simone de Beauvoir's definition. And I accept that these women's

*The name Simone de Beauvoir is known by to all her old friends.

groups must exist. I only said that in my view their refusal to hold mixed meetings is not always justified. There could be meetings that men could participate in. I think that women do indeed – if you like – represent a particular kind of oppressed people; they are oppressed in a specific way. That has nothing to do with the working class. And, incidentally, the nature of the oppression is not the same. Workers are oppressed in a particular way and women are oppressed in their way, even when they are not working-class women! Neither the form of the oppression nor its extent are the same. So I believe that the relationship between a woman and a man, or a man and a woman, as you like, is in fact a relationship of oppression. But I don't see what more I can do than denounce this state of affairs.

s. de b.] It must also be said in this context that he has done a great deal of propaganda work among his colleagues on *La Libération* to persuade them to take women on to the paper and to concern themselves with women's problems, for example, and they have also done some very good pieces on abortion – and he has even been trying to cure them of their *machismo*. He has been battling against his young colleagues' *machismo* because being on the extreme left does not make the majority of them any less macho, in varying degrees and in a more or less subtle way.

Rome, 1973

'The Second Sex': thirty years on

ALICE SCHWARZER] Five years have passed since you first stated that you were a feminist. You, the writer who had been the greatest source of inspiration for the new feminism, had actually been an anti-feminist until the new women's movement started, in the sense that you opposed an autonomous women's movement, and believed that the socialist revolution would automatically resolve the question of women's oppression. A great deal has happened since then. You are active in the women's movement yourself, and the women's struggle has entered public awareness. So-called International Women's Year seems symptomatic of that. What do you think?

SIMONE DE BEAUVOIR] We feminists have often said what we think of that. We have been made fools of and have been humiliated. The next thing will be an International Year of the Sea, then an International Year of the Horse, the Dog and so on ... In other words, people think of women as objects that are not worth taking seriously for more than a year in this man's world. And yet we make up half of the human race. So it follows that it is absolutely grotesque to talk of *an* International Women's Year. Every year ought to be International Women's Year, in fact International People's Year ...

A. S.] But all the same, don't you think that − in complete contrast to the original intentions of those who initiated it − the open cynicism with which most men have celebrated International Women's Year has been an outrage to many women, and that the women's struggle has been strengthened as a result?

S. de B.] I do not think we have International Women's Year to thank for that; it was the efforts of the women's movement; i.e. women with no organised or official status. International Women's Year only came about because of the women's movement. And with the intention of taking over the women's movement, so to speak. To calm the waves. The Year itself has not brought us any further forward. Those women in Mexico were nothing more than puppets of male politics. That could be seen most clearly in the clash between the women representing Israel and those representing the Arab countries. They are both as patriarchal as each other, and Islam probably even more so than Judaism. A. S.] All the same, couldn't one say that International Women's Year was of some value, despite everything? S. de B.] Of course. Basically, it has to be said that even quite miserable reforms always have some value but that they are dangerous as well. The best example is the new French Abortion Law. It is a completely inadequate measure which only came about in response to our struggle. That was M. Giscard d'Estaing's doing, in his desire to be modern, i.e. he does not attack actual privileges, but just scratches the surface of some things that are taboo. Fine. So it is a measure which in one sense does not signify any fundamental change. It is entirely consistent with a capitalist, patriarchal world (the best evidence of that is that there is also free abortion in the United States and Japan). But still one should not underestimate a reform of this kind. It makes many acute problems easier for women, and it is a beginning as well. Just like the Pill was. But like the Pill, which endangers women's health and which puts increasing pressure on women to take sole responsiblity for contraception, free abortion could also easily rebound on us too. In a male dominated world, a male backlash is only to be expected. Men will use it as an additional means of applying pressure. They will say, 'Come on, there's no danger now, you can let me. You can always have an abortion . . .'

A. S.] In 1971 you were one of the women who publicly admitted to having had an abortion. Since then you have taken part in various feminist initiatives and campaigns. What is your relationship with young feminists like today?

S. de B.] I have personal relations with individual women, not with groups or factions. I work with them on specific projects. For example, on *Les Temps Modernes* we do a regular page together on 'Everyday Sexism'. Apart from that, I am the president of the 'League for Women's Rights', and I support efforts to set up homes for battered women. So I'm not a militant in the strict sense – after all, I'm not thirty any more, I'm sixty-seven, an intellectual whose weapons are her words – but I follow the activities of the women's movement at very close hand, and I am at its disposal.

I consider this project for battered women to be of great importance, because, like the problem of abortion, the problem of violence affects nearly all women – regardless of their social class. It is not restricted to any one class. Women are beaten by husbands who are judges or presiding magistrates as well as by husbands who are labourers. So we have now founded an 'SOS Battered Women', and we are trying to get houses so that we can offer at least temporary shelter for a night or a few weeks to a woman – and her children – who risks being battered, sometimes to death.

A. S.] You have taught the new feminists a great deal. Have they taught you anything?

S. de B.] Yes! A great deal! They have radicalised me in

many of my views! Personally, I have got used to living in a world in which men are what they are, namely oppressors. Personally I have not really suffered from it all that much. I've escaped most of the usual kinds of female slave labour, I have never been a mother or a housewife.

Nowadays feminists refuse to be token women, like I was. And they're right! One must fight! The main thing they've taught me is vigilance, and not to let anything pass, not even the most trivial things like this ordinary sexism we've got so used to. It starts at the level of grammar, where the masculine always comes before the feminine.

A. S.] Most men on the left have internalised their 'superiority complex' (as you yourself once called it) to such a degree that they go on treating feminists, who have always seen themselves as part of the left, as 'petites bourgeoises' or 'reactionary'. They see the sex war as a 'secondary contradiction' dividing the working class, the 'primary contradiction'.

S. de B.] The poor things. They can't help it. Even left-wingers are chauvinists. It's in their blood . . . this is another of those male mystifications. The contradiction between man and woman is just as primary and just as fundamental as any other. After all, it's one half of humanity against the other half. To me, it seems just as important as the class struggle. This is a very complicated matter, and the MLF will have to find a link between the two.

And, in any case, nowadays, the idea that the class struggle takes priority is increasingly being called into question at various levels, even on the left, because one can see there are any number of struggles which go beyond the bounds of the class struggle. For example, the foreign workers' struggle, the struggle of French soldiers in barracks, and the struggle of young people ... and especially the women's struggle, which is not specific to any one class.

Of course, the oppression of women takes on different forms, according to class. There are women who are victims on both fronts: working women who are themselves workers' wives. Others only suffer female oppression, in the sense that they are mothers and housewives. But even middle-class women, when their husbands abandon them, drop down to the proletariat very quickly. There they are – no jobs, no qualifications, no money of their own ... to deny which is another male trick to confine things to the struggles between men. The most that women – these treasures – are asked to do is to lend a hand now and again. It's a bit like the relationship between blacks and whites.

A. S.] *The Second Sex*, still the bible of feminism, so to speak, with over a million copies sold in America alone, was originally a purely intellectual and theoretical work. What were reactions like when it came out in 1949?

S. de B.] Very violent! Very, very hostile, to the book and to me.

A. S.] From which quarter?

S. de B.] From all quarters. But perhaps we made a mistake in publishing the chapter on sexuality in *Les Temps Modernes* before the book actually came out. That was the beginning of the storm. And the vulgarity ... Mauriac, for example, immediately wrote to one of our friends who was working with us at *Les Temps Modernes* at the time: 'Oh, I have just learned a lot about your employer's vagina ...'

And Camus, who was still a friend then, bellowed, 'You have made a laughing-stock of the French male!' Some professors threw the book across their offices because they couldn't bear to read it.

And when I went into a restaurant, to La Coupole, say, dressed in a more feminine way, as is my style, people would stare and say, 'Ah, so that's her . . . I thought that . . . she must be both ways then . . .' Because at the time, I was generally reputed to be a lesbian. A woman who dares to say such things simply cannot be 'normal'.

Even the Communists tore me to shreds. They accused me of being a 'petite bourgeoise' and told me, 'You see, what you are saying really doesn't mean a thing to working-class women in Billancourt' – which is completely and utterly untrue. I had neither the right nor the left on my side.

A. S.] Some even went as far as to say that Sartre had written your books, not you. And in any case, as far as male-dominated public opinion is concerned, you have always been the 'relative being' that you denounced in *The Second Sex*, the woman who only exists in relation to a man, namely as 'Sartre's life companion'. Describing Sartre as 'de Beauvoir's life companion' would have been unthinkable!

S. de B.] Exactly. In France particularly, their rage knew no bounds. Things were better abroad, because it's easier to tolerate a foreigner. It's a long way away, and therefore less of a threat.

A. S.] I know that for the last thirty years you have been getting letters every day from women the world over. Even before the new collective women's struggles came into existence, Simone, you were an idol for many of them, and you still embody our revolt. Without a doubt this results from your profound analysis of the position of women, and your autobiographical novels as well, because they have portrayed a woman with the courage to exist. Have you learned anything new from these letters?

s. de b.] I have come to understand the enormous extent of oppression! There are some women who are actually imprisoned! And it is by no means uncommon. They write to me in secret, before their husbands come home. The most interesting letters come from women between thirty-five and forty-five who are married and used to be very happy, but are now at a dead end . . . they ask me, 'What can I do? I have no professional training. I have nothing. I am nothing.'

At eighteen or twenty you get married for love, and at thirty it all hits you – and getting out of that situation is very, very difficult. It could have happened to me, which is why I feel particularly sensitive to it.

a. s.] Giving advice is always a delicate matter, but if a woman does ask you . . .

s. de b.] I think a woman should be on her guard against the trap of motherhood and marriage. Even if she would dearly like to have children, she ought to think seriously about the conditions under which she would have to bring them up, because being a mother these days is real slavery. Fathers and society leave sole responsibility for the children to the mother. Women give up their jobs to look after small children. Women stay at home when the child has measles. And women are blamed if the child doesn't succeed.

If a woman still wants a child in spite of everything, it would be better to have one without getting married, because marriage is really the biggest trap of all.

A. s.] But what if women are already married and already have children?

s. de B.] In the interview with you four years ago,* I said that a housewife of thirty-five or more really didn't stand much of a chance. Subsequently I had a lot of nice letters from women who said, 'But that's not true at all! We can still put up a very good fight!' So much the better. But whatever else, they should attempt to find a paid job so that they at least have some measure of independence and a chance to stand on their own two feet.

A. s.] And housework? What about that? Should women refuse to do more housework and bringing up children than men do?

s. de B.] Yes, but that's not enough. We must find new ways of doing things for the future. Women should not be the only ones to do housework – everybody should. And, above all, it should not be done in such isolation!

I don't mean special groups to do the work, the way it used to be done in the Soviet Union at one time. That seems very dangerous to me, because it means there are people who spend their entire lives sweeping floors or ironing. That is not a solution.

What I do think is very good is what apparently happens in certain parts of China, where everybody – men, women, even children – get together on a particular day to make housework a public activity, which can also be a lot of fun. So they all get together to do the washing or the cleaning, or whatever.

There is no job which is degrading in itself. All jobs are of equal value. The degrading thing is working conditions. What's wrong with cleaning windows? It's just as

*See p. 39.

useful as typing. What is degrading is the conditions under which the windows are cleaned.

Solitude, boredom, non-productivity, no integration into a collective. That is what's bad! As is the division of labour into private/public. Everything ought to be public, so to speak!

A. S.] Some members of the women's movement – and indeed some people in the political parties – are calling for wages for housework . . .

S. de B.] I'm completely and utterly opposed to that! Of course! In the short term, maybe housewives who have no alternative would be glad of a wage. That is understandable. But in the long term, it would encourage women to believe that being a housewife was a job and an acceptable way of life. But being banished to the ghetto of domesticity and the division of labour along male/female, private/public lines is precisely what women should be rejecting if they want to realise their full value as human beings. So I am against wages for housework.

A. S.] Some women argue that their demanding wages for housework would create an awareness of the value of housework.

S. de B.] I agree. But I don't think that is the right way to do it. The thing to change is the conditions of housework. Otherwise its value will continue to be associated with the isolation of women, which is something I think should be rejected. Men must be made to share the housework, and it should be done publicly. It must be integrated into the community and the collectives where everybody works together. That's the way it's done in some primitive societies, incidentally, where the family is not synonymous with isolation. The family ghetto must be destroyed!

A. S.] You yourself, Simone, have solved the problem on an individual basis. You don't have any children and you and Sartre don't live together – in other words, you have never done any housework for a family or for a man. You have often been attacked for your attitude to motherhood – by women as well as men. They accuse you of being against motherhood.

S. de B.] Oh no! I do not reject motherhood. I just think that these days motherhood is a very nasty trap for women. I wouldn't advise a woman to have children for that very reason. But I am not making a value judgement.

I'm not against mothers, but the ideology which expects every woman to have children, and I'm against the circumstances under which mothers have to have their children.

Then, too, there is a dreadful mystification of the mother-child relationship. I think the reason people place so much value on the family and children is because they generally live such lonely lives. They have no friends, no love, no affection. They are alone. So they have children for the sake of having someone. And that is terrible, for the child as well. It becomes a stop-gap to fill up this emptiness. And then as soon as the child is grown up, he leaves home anyway. A child is no guarantee against loneliness.

A. S.] You have often been asked if you now regret not having had children?

S. de B.] Oh no! I congratulate myself every day on it. When I see grandmothers who have to look after small children – instead of finally having a bit of time to themselves – it's not always sheer pleasure for them.

A. S.] What role do you think that sexuality, as it is understood today, plays in the oppression of women?

s. de b.] I think that sexuality can be a dreaful trap. Some women become frigid – but that is perhaps not the worst thing that can happen to them. The worst thing is for women to find sexuality so enjoyable that they become more or less slaves to men – which can be another link in the chain shackling women to men.

a. s.] If I understand you correctly, you see frigidity, given the current state of malaise created by the power relationships between men and women, as a more cautious and more appropriate reaction, because it reflects this unease, and makes women less dependent on men?

s. de b.] Exactly.

a. s.] There are women in the women's movement who refuse to continue to share their private lives with men in this male-dominated world, i.e. they do not have sexual or emotional relationships with men. In other words, women who have made a political strategy out of their female homosexuality. What do you think of that?

s. de b.] I have a lot of understanding for this political refusal to compromise, precisely for the reason I have just indicated. Love can be a trap which makes women put up with a great deal.

But this seems to me right only under present circumstances. In itself, female homosexuality is just as restricting as heterosexuality. The ideal thing would be to be able to love a woman just as well as a man, a human being pure and simple, without fear, without pressure, without obligations.

a. s.] Your most famous statement is 'One is not born, but rather becomes, a woman.' Nowadays, it's possible to prove this 'shaping' of the sexes, and the result is that women and men are very different: they think differently, they have different emotions, they walk differently. They were not born like that, but they have become like that. It's the result of their education and their daily lives.

Almost everybody agrees that this difference exists. But this difference is not just a difference: it also implies the inferiority of women. In this context it is particularly remarkable that a renaissance of the eternal feminine, a general mystification of the feminine, is appearing at the same time as the new female revolt.

s. de b.] I think that today certain male failings are absent in women. For example, that grotesque masculine way of taking themselves seriously, their vanity, their self-importance. It's true that women who have a male career can easily acquire these failings too. But all the same, they do retain something of a sense of humour and tend to keep a healthy distance from hierarchies.

And then the habit of putting down all the competition – generally women don't do that. And patience – which can be a virtue up to a certain point, though after that it becomes a weakness – is also a female characteristic. And a sense of irony. And a straightforward manner, since women have their feet on the ground because of the role they play in daily life.

These 'feminine' qualities are a product of our oppression, but they ought to be retained after our liberation. And men would have to learn to acquire them. But we shouldn't go to the other extreme and say that a woman has a particular closeness with the earth, that she feels the rhythm of the moon, the ebb and flow of the tides . . . Or that she has more soul, or is less destructive by nature etc. No! If there is a grain of truth in that, it is not because of our nature, but is rather the result of our conditions of existence.

Those little girls who are so 'feminine' are made, not born, that way. Any number of studies have proved that. A woman has no particular value *a priori* simply because she is a woman. That would be the most sinister biological distortion, and in total contradiction to everything I think.

A. S.] So what does this renaissance of the 'eternal feminine' really signify?

s. de B.] When men tell us, 'Just go on being a good little woman. Leave all the irksome things like power, honour, careers to us . . . Be glad that you are as you are, in tune with the earth, preoccupied with human concerns . . .', it is really very dangerous. On the one hand, it's right that women no longer feel ashamed about their bodies, about pregnancy, about menstruation. I think it's excellent for women to get to know their own bodies.

But one should not make it a value in itself either; one should not believe that the female body gives one a new vision of the world. That would be ridiculous and absurd. That would mean turning it into a counter-penis. Women who believe that are descending to the level of the irrational, the mystical, the cosmic. They are playing the men's game, which allows men to oppress women all the more as a result, and keep them away from knowledge and power with more success.

The 'eternal feminine' is a lie because nature plays only a tiny part in the development of a human being; we are social beings. Furthermore, just as I do not believe that women are inferior to men by nature, nor do I believe that they are their natural superiors either.

Paris, 1976

'Women have less far to fall'

ALICE SCHWARZER] You have not only analysed the situation of women in *The Second Sex*, but also studied *Old Age*, as one of your works is called. Today is your seventieth birthday. According to your own criteria, you are yourself old. How do you feel?

SIMONE DE BEAUVOIR] The same as ever. Today is no different just because I am seventy. Of course, seventy is a round figure, but it weighs no more heavily on me than sixty-nine or sixty-eight or sixty . . . I realised a long time ago that I was not young any more. When I was fifty, it was a real shock for me to hear young women say, 'Oh well, Simone de Beauvoir is an old woman.' Or sometimes they would say, to my face, 'Goodness, you really remind me of my mother . . .' I am seventy now and for the last twenty years I have been used to not being young any more, and to not seeing myself as young either. But since I don't have much of a self-image and don't think about myself as a person very much – although, on the other hand, I do think a lot about the world around me – age really doesn't bother me at all.

A. S.] That is what I thought from reading your memoirs and looking at your photos. If growing old ever came as a shock to you, it was more likely to have been in your fifties . . .

S. de B.] Exactly. Because it coincided with a very sombre period in French history. It was the time of the Algerian war. I was overwhelmed by the course of events. I thought I was getting old and that the political future was overcast at one and the same time. That all led to the sad and disillusioned ending to *Force of Circumstance*. But since then I have got used to it all.

A. S.] At the time you were bitterly attacked, especially by women, for that sentence, 'J'ai été flouée' [I have been cheated]. As well as being the author of *The Second Sex* you have become something of a symbol of their emancipation. As a result, many of them cast you in the role of professional optimist.

s. de b.] Exactly.

a. s.] You are expected to implement and achieve everything women find very difficult to live out in practice today. In *Old Age*, you wrote, 'I refuse to be alienated from myself by a fixed image', and say that you place your personal freedom above your political interests.

s. de b.] Yes, and that is very important to me.

a. s.] In *Old Age* you describe the 'dignity' old people are expected to have as a factor of their oppression. It's the same thing for women; people want to deny them passion or a sense of revolt in the name of their dignity. But you have never bowed to these expectations. Were you an 'undignified old lady'?

s. de b.] No, not at all. Brecht's 'undignified old lady' was a woman who had repressed her desires all her life and then really let rip. I on the other hand have always spoken my mind as far as I have been able. I have always followed my desires and my impulses; in other words, I didn't suppress anything, so that I have no need to get even with my past now.

a. s.] Is there anything you did not write in your memoirs which you would say now, if you had to write them again?

s. de b.] Yes. I would have liked to have given a frank and balanced account of my own sexuality. A truly sincere one, from a feminist point of view; I would like to tell women about my life in terms of my own sexuality because it is not just a personal matter but a political one too. I did not write about it at the time because I did not appreciate the importance of this question, nor the need for personal honesty. And I am very unlikely to write about it now because this kind of confession would not just affect me, it would also affect certain people who are very close to me.

A. S.] Sexuality is necessarily a taboo subject for old people, too. You have made that extremely clear in your essay. How have you reacted to this? Have you bowed to this taboo?

S. de B.] To some extent, I have always submitted. Not to the taboos, but to my head. Because I think my head has always exerted a stronger pull on me than my body. Perhaps there was a degree of hysteria involved; at times when there was no possibility of a sexual life, I did not feel sexual desire. In fact, the only desires I ever had were always linked to a specific person and capable of realisation; and if that was not possible, for one reason or another, I did not feel sexual desire.

In fact, sexuality has always gone hand in hand with love for me, except perhaps when I was very young. When I was twelve, I thought, 'Heavens, do I really have to wait until I am fifteen to get married?' That seemed terrible to me! At that time, I was prey to an over-whelming sexual urge, without knowing what it meant. I felt, even if only vaguely, that I needed a body, caresses, something. But that was just about the only time in my life when I experienced sexuality in this unfocussed way.

Today, that is all over and done with. Something in my body is dead. And so much the better. I have no objections to old women who are still overcome by sexual desire, but I do think they have a damned difficult time of it.

A. S.] In *Old Age* you talk about the bodies of old

people with a certain distaste. Are you now finding your own body similarly repellent?

s. de b.] You know, I have never been very vain. I have never derived much pleasure from my own body. So obviously it is only to be expected that I am even less happy with it now.

a. s.] You have always been a very beautiful woman, by male standards. Has losing your looks bothered you?

s. de b.] I never set too much store by good looks. People have been kind enough to say that they found me attractive. When I was thirty, thirty-five, forty, I sometimes looked in the mirror and quite liked what I saw. But it has never been the obsession for me that it is for some women to whom looks are everything, and who have a lot of difficulty coming to terms with growing old. To me the most important thimg was my mind, everything else took second place.

All the same, I took a certain pleasure in my face, and when I compared it at fifty or fifty-two with the way it had been at forty, and saw the change, I was not very happy. But I have got used to it, and as you can imagine, this is a question which no longer arises.

a. s.] In *Old Age* you describe the conflict between the objective state of old age and one's subjective feelings. You say, 'One feels young in an old body.'

s. de b.] I certainly think there is a discrepancy. Sartre defined old age very well when he described it as 'the unrealisable'. It is a state that obtains for other people, but not so much for oneself. When I wake up, when I walk or read a book, I never think of myself as being any special age. In fact, I don't think of myself as any age at all, just as one doesn't think of age when one is young. On the other hand, there are times when one is fully aware of it. In *The Mandarins*, and in *Force of Circumstance* too, I talked about the time when the heroine starts to tell herself, 'I am old.' But I don't tell myself now, I know. This is a feeling which has become second nature to my habits and my body, and yet I still don't see myself as an old woman. Cocteau put it neatly when he said the bad thing about growing old is staying young.

A. S.] But hasn't old age affected your daily life?

S. de B.] Yes. It is a little difficult to explain. But I would say that I do not feel as strong as I used to.

When I was thirty, I was up and about as soon as I opened my eyes, racing about, working, doing all sorts of different things. Nowadays, I like to take my time and to relax. I enjoy putting my feet up during the day and reading and just being quiet. And then there are some things today which don't have any meaning or attraction for me any more, even though I enjoyed them so much when I was forty. Going out, for instance. Or evenings spent drinking and chatting with friends.

I think in particular of the time after the war when we were still relatively young and were celebrating the Liberation. We planned all sorts of projects together. That was a very potent and a very happy time. But circumstances do not lend themselves now in the same way, and I am very well aware that my body is not up to it either. In those days, as soon as I woke up, I rushed to my desk. I had already started writing before I had even had a cup of tea. It was a passion, and it was a very enjoyable life.

Nowadays, I don't feel I have all that much left to do. In one sense, I am glad. It means a certain amount of leisure and a degree of freedom. I wouldn't say that I live more according to whim exactly, but I can act according to my mood at any moment. I am less set on the future than I used to be. At the same time though, I regret that, because that feeling does mean that one sensed a future ahead of one. All the same, in my view, the most radiant period in one's life is between thirty and fifty, when one has set the framework of one's life and one is free of the constraints of youth – family matters, career pressures – it is the time when one is free and there is a lot to come. But old age means taking a step out of the infinite into the finite. One has no future – that is the worst thing.

A. S.] Does the fact that you have a body of work behind you and that you have done so many things take the edge off growing old?

S. de B.] Certainly. It does make it easier for me, but it makes it worse too. I say to myself, 'All right, perhaps I could write one or two more books, but the bulk of my work is behind me.'

A. S.] What projects do you have now?

S. de B.] At the moment, the thing that interests me and which I am really enjoying is something I have never done before – the filming of my books. It is not a new thing as such, but it is a new way of making things I have already written more accessible to the public. I worked on the filming of *The Woman Destroyed*, for example. There may also be a major series on *The Mandarins*. Basically I feel a need to go over my work and to give it a new meaning, in order to reach a public not used to reading, but to watching television. In other words, a public different to the one I have had hitherto. I could get fed up with it, but that's what interests me just now. Perhaps in two years time it will be something else. But there's something else I would very much like to do if I were thirty or forty now, and that is a work on psychoanalysis.

I would not take Freud as my starting point, but go right back to basics and from a feminist perspective, from a feminine rather than a masculine viewpoint. But I shan't do it. I don't have enough time ahead of me. Other women will have to do it.

A. S.] I would like to come back to *Old Age*. You wrote the book when you were sixty and on the threshold of your own old age, and you quote a striking number of examples of writers or artists coming to grips with their own old age. Was it a way of finding out what was in store for you yourself?

S. de B.] No, not at all. It's true that the subject appealed to me, inasmuch as I was starting to grow old myself. But it was not that so much which made me write the book. The problem was just beginning to be discussed – I didn't invent it. People are living longer than they used to, and old people's living conditions are simply appalling. I knew about their economic and social problems at close quarters through women friends of mine who work in the social services, and through everything one reads. I felt concern and sympathy for old people, I wanted to talk about it.

At the same time of course, I was particularly interested to know what the experience of people in my circle, writers and artists, was like at this period in their lives. And that was the part of the book that I enjoyed most: reading what old people have written and thought about their own old age.

A. S.] Has the fact that you have analysed old age had an effect on your own life?

S. de B.] No.

A. S.] That surprises me. To be aware of one's situation usually means some changes to it. That is what happens to women when they become aware of their own situation. It makes some things easier – because one is not alone with it any more and has more understanding – and some things more difficult, because one sees things all too clearly.

s. de b.] No, that is really not the case for me with my own old age. Nothing can take the place of actual experience. The fact that I have written a theoretical book on the subject neither discourages nor encourages me. It may be that I recognise certain traits more easily in other people. But not in myself. Two years ago, I had such a terrible attack of rheumatism that I had to stay in bed, and afterwards I could not get upstairs so easily. But I really didn't need to have written a book on old age to know that physical feebleness has something to do with it.

a. s.] Poverty is one of the major problems of old age. You are privileged from that point of view.

s. de b.] That's certainly true.

a. s.] There is yet another problem of old age that you are spared. I'm thinking of loneliness.

s. de b.] Yes, that's true. I have many friends and some warm and intimate relationships with a few people. Not very many: I do not want many, I want to be able to give fairly of myself to these relationships. Even if two or three of the people most dear to me were to die at the same time, in an air crash, say, I know there would always be someone close to me. No, I will never be alone until the day I die.

a. s.] Although people predicted that as an unmarried woman without any children you would be lonely in your old age.

s. de b.] Yes. One of the many predictions that never came true . . .

a. s.] Apart from Sartre, there is someone else who plays a very important role in your life – Sylvie, with whom you have been close friends for many years. Is Sylvie a sort of substitute daughter?

s. de b.] Absolutely not!

a. s.] How so?

s. de b.] Mother-daughter relationships are generally catastrophic. A mother cannot play the role of mother and that of friend at the same time. She may well want to. But her daughter will desert her very quickly. She will come to love her again, but in a different way. And that happens because a child doesn't want to hang around in the womb for ever. The mother-daughter relationships I see around me are bearable at best, never really passionate or loving, which is what I think relationships ought to be.

a. s.] And your relationship with Sylvie?

s. de b.] That is different. We first met when we were both grown-up people, and we chose each other freely. A profound understanding has developed between us. It is true that her youth rejuvenates me, but that's not why we became friends. It was not calculated in any way.

a. s.] Do you think that old age is more difficult for women than for men?

s. de b.] No, I don't, and I said so in *Old Age*. Being old is much more difficult for men, in fact. Because we women – and I am not talking about myself, because I am in a very privileged position in this respect, but women in general – we have less far to fall. We have always been kept down to a low level.

But men who are generally full of their own importance, who believe they have power and responsibility; when they grow old, it's really terrible! It's a complete break. Women geriatric specialists have told me that they see men in their fifties who are completely broken: they cannot take in the fact that their twenty-five-year-old sons are usurping them, and they are absolutely shattered. By contrast, a woman can still have a role to play.

Not that I like the way things are for women these days, but it does give them a few more opportunities to escape. That is one advantage we have. Women have always been put down, they have never had any power, and when they suddenly see their husbands stripped of all their power, they quite often turn the tables on them. It's not always very endearing behaviour, but it does make things easier for them. And I understand that very well.

A. S.] Isn't it also because men are locked in permanent conflict and rivalry? So, obviously, growing old and losing an income is doubly hazardous for them.

S. de B.] Exactly. They do not have anything else. Whereas in their old age women still have their function in the house. I don't like the fact that women's activities centre on the home, cooking and looking after their grandchildren – things that are very limited in scope, as they have been all their lives. But all the same, it is a practical, psychological resource which enables them to survive much better.

A. S.] In that sense, you yourself are in more of a male situation, and indeed in an extremely privileged one. Has the fact that you are famous, or rather the fact that through your work you have made such a distinctive contribution to the development of awareness and emancipation of so many women, and that you are loved and admired by millions of women, has this fact had an effect on your private life?

s. de b.] No. Except that I receive more letters and manuscripts from feminists than I used to. At the same time though, now and again I get the odd one from some young feminist who finds Simone de Beauvoir's brand of feminism old hat. I find it quite normal. One should always challenge and reject. Apart from that though, there are other things to be done now than to write *The Second Sex*. Having said that, I think that *The Second Sex* remains a very valuable basis and feminists openly make use of it. So I'm not ashamed, nor especially pleased, at being recognised as a professional feminist.

a. s.] In any case, you and Sartre gave young people enough encouragement to protest.

s. de b.] That's true. So it does not bother me at all. And anyway, you never see yourself as an idol. I am Simone de Beauvoir for other people, not for myself.

Paris, 1978

'A vote against this world'

ALICE SCHWARZER] As feminists we plead the cause of autonomy for the women's movement, although in my opinion that should not mean women abstaining from positions of influence in society. What do you think?

SIMONE DE BEAUVOIR] I'm hesitant ... Of course, you can always achieve something if you have power. Only – what? A woman in a position of power comes to resemble a man. She becomes a sort of token woman, and as such does men's work for them and even more effectively and more discreetly, like Françoise Giroud, for example.*

A. S.] This is the kind of bitter experience we're having in West Germany. That's why I'm not asking the question so much in terms of individual women who make their way into positions of power in dribs and drabs, but more in terms of groups and movements which could become a power factor in the political sphere – without necessarily becoming an integral part of the political process. By applying pressure from without, for example.

S. DE B.] Yes, but then they really mustn't play by the rules of those who do have power, as token women do.

A. S.] And what is your attitude to the idea of a women's party, as has been suggested in West Germany?

S. DE B.] I find it simply absurd. For a start, it wouldn't stand a chance and its only value would be symbolic. And secondly, because being a woman is not enough in itself. A woman president would do exactly the same as a man president would do in her place. For example, there hasn't been a noticeable outbreak of social justice under

*Giscard d'Estaing's former Secretary of State for Women's Questions.

Mrs Thatcher's government ... So it cannot be a question of power for its own sake and at any price.

A. S.] All the same, I think it's important to take a closer look at the idea of a women's party, because many women see it as a very promising path ...

S. de B.] ... which is bound to take them up a blind alley. Anyway, what is the term 'women's party' supposed to mean? After all, where politics are concerned, we don't want to restrict ourselves to the ghetto of the women's problem, we want to take part in discussions about everything. It's not just a question of women's problems. And I also think that with a carbon copy of the existing system – except that instead of a male-dominated party, there is a party in which women have the power – one is sticking too closely to the existing rules of the game. And the existing rules of the game are always those of the people in power. We must put a brake on the machinery of power, rather than go on oiling its wheels. We must fight against the exploitation of women in all areas, not declare ourselves content with any one party. There is the question of housework for example. In economic terms, this is invisible work for which women are not even paid. It would be marvellous if there was a revolt against this work! Or against unequal pay. At the same time we must fight against the stereotyping of women in the role of housewife and mother, against the fact that women sacrifice themselves for that more than for anything else.

A. S.] Elections are due to take place shortly in West Germany and France. Should we feminists continue to behave as we always have done in the past – waking up at the last minute, a couple of weeks before votes are cast, and quickly firing off a few broadsides, which are often pathetic and generally ineffective? Or should we not use this situation to make our problems public, to become a power factor that cannot be left out of all the political wrangling that goes on, and to wring a few minor concessions out of the parties competing for our votes?

s. de b.] Why not? But it shouldn't stop at finding out the intentions of parties and candidates, because that is playing their game. As we know from experience, these gentlemen are easily able to make promises today which they cannot keep tomorrow. And anyway, should one vote for a party just because it promises something on this point or that? I detest this kind of horse-trading. Don't you?

a. s.] I think . . . In principle, I find your position of consistent rigour correct. Only there are times when I could see some tactical sense in saying, you scratch my back, I'll scratch yours. At the same time, one must make it clear that by no means is one handing a party a blank cheque.

s. de b.] I consider that dangerous. On the other hand . . . I have behaved like that often enough in my life, voted against my better judgement – simply because I hoped for some slight improvement. For example, in the last election anything was better than Giscard, as far as I was concerned. The Popular Front, for instance. But then I have such a horror of the French Communist Party and find the way it toes the Moscow line repulsive . . . That left the socialists, who might be the lesser evil. There were even some women in their ranks who would probably work for our cause. But in the main, the socialists would presumably feel an obligation to represent the interests of the workers and other disadvantaged people a little better.

I am not saying this as a feminist, by the way. We women cannot expect anything more from them either. I am simply saying that in the context of a certain humanism of a general kind . . .

A. S.] In West Germany as well, much is said about the 'lesser evil' in connection with the socialists, so-called . . .

S. de B.] . . . They are no more than so-called socialists here too.

A. S.] Yes, but all the same a bit more so than the SPD, the Social Democratic Party of Germany, large parts of which are more directly comparable to the left and centre wings of the Gaullists than to the French Socialists . . . But it's precisely these general humanitarian considerations which always get us in the end! In fact, our 'lesser evil', the SPD, relies on just that! Don't you find these ostensible alternatives – either being passive or resigning oneself to the so-called lesser evil – highly unsatisfactory too?

S. de B.] Yes. Only I can't see how we can change things. We would have to develop an offensive strategy to break through it. From outside of course! So the only possible course seems to be an election boycott, and for that we need a broad political movement. Otherwise, not voting is going to be seen as an admission of defeat.

An election boycott does not mean being passive, in fact one must become active. One must say why one is calling these parties and the principle of parliament into question. One mustn't just sit around at home. One should go to the polling station and spoil one's ballot paper or vote 'no'. That is the only way to avoid the danger of an election boycott having a rebound effect, which would only be of value to the right. A boycott must be a quite conscious vote: a vote against the world as it exists! A vote against what passes for politics in the existing system! A vote against the way women and their interests are totally ignored!

A. S.] What has your own attitude been towards this question at various stages in your life? You haven't always been so critical of the parties, have you? At the beginning of the fifties you voted Communist, and before the Second World War you were fairly apolitical, weren't you?

S. de B.] That's not quite the case. Although I wasn't active before the war, I was very interested in politics. Sartre and I were delighted about the victory of the Popular Front in 1936. But we were spectators, not participants, at their demonstrations. Of course, we made donations to the strikers, and our hearts beat for the left. But we stopped there. We had no tactics. And as far as elections were concerned — as a woman I did not even have the right to vote.* And Sartre did not vote on principle. He loathes elections.

A. S.] What about after the Second World War?

S. de B.] I sometimes voted Communist. And then I was very active in certain political campaigns: against the colonial wars, against the war in Indo-China, against the Algerian war (which was never called that publicly) — but of course we could not articulate protest at elections because all the parties let us down on these key issues. Just take Algeria — it was betrayed by the Socialists just as much as by the Communists. We had to fight against the Algerian war from the outside, from the sidelines, from underground. And similarly women will probably also

*Women in France did not get the vote until after the Second World War.

have to fight from the outside, in the areas where they really want fundamental change.

A. S.] Which takes us back to the original question: how do we start?

S. de B.] Exactly. It is perhaps a particularly difficult decision because obviously there is more chance of some slight progress if the Socialists are at the helm, rather than the Conservatives.

A. S.] And then our grand principles and our small daily lives tend to collide . . .

S. de B.] . . . and that is why I always find myself wavering. For example, if I thought that pensions and minimum wages would be increased a little under certain governments, or that workers and trades unions would have a few more rights etc. – then I would prefer that government to any other, despite my deep-seated misgivings, and my fundamental objection to parliamentary democracy, which does not exist, as can be seen by the almost total absence of women in parliaments and governments.

A. S.] And that takes us back to the horse-trading. Although it seems to me that it would be a step forward if more women, and indeed people in general, were to recognise this horse-trading for what it is – in other words, if we finally stopped issuing blank cheques to parties and started keeping a very close eye on them. In fact, in the last few years there have been signs that people are becoming disillusioned with parties. At this stage, decisive action is essential – by which I mean finding effective forms of protest so as to prevent a sense of resignation which can then be exploited. And the dangers of manipulation should not be underestimated. You can see that in the so-called 'new femininity', which actually hampers the emancipation of women, rather than helping it.

s. de b.] I see things in exactly the same way. At the moment, unfortunately, it is more a matter of a step backwards than a step forwards. The main reason for that here in France is that the government has been clever enough to adopt some of the demands made by women. So now there are women in the elite schools, whereas previously they were barred from them, there is even a woman in the *Académie Française* – we are being given the illusion that a woman can achieve anything today, and that it is her fault if she does not. It all goes hand-in-hand with this so-called 'new femininity' – with an enhanced status for traditional feminine values, such as woman and her rapport with nature, woman and her maternal instinct, woman and her physical being (some even go as far as saying that 'Women write with their wombs') etc. This renewed attempt to pin women down to their traditional role, together with a small effort to meet some of the demands made by women – that's the formula used to try and keep women quiet. And unfortunately, as one can see from the tragic results, it is a really successful approach. Even women who call themselves feminists don't always see through it. Once again, women are being defined in terms of 'the other', once again they are being made into the 'second sex'.

a. s.] That seems to me to be the precise background against which the new women's peace movements are emerging. Mostly with the best of intentions, of course, because what decent person is not for peace? Women and peace – it's the same old story, and one that is primarily designed to suggest our pacific qualities.

s. de b.] Why should women be more in favour of peace

than men? I should think it a matter of equal concern for both! And furthermore, can anyone nowadays seriously believe that petitions and rallies can really do anything to advance the cause of peace? That really is utter rubbish. To maintain or attain peace, one must fight for it. And fight for it where decisions about war and peace are made! The argument that women are so willing to accept, namely, 'We do not want to provide the cannon-fodder', only applies to women who are mothers. So being a mother means being for peace. The Greens use similar arguments. Equating ecology with feminism is something that irritates me. They are not automatically one and the same thing at all.

A. S.] Once again, it is the sexist definition of women as beings who are closer to nature than men . . .

S. de B.] That's it. These are attempts to divert women from their struggle for emancipation, and to channel their energies into subsidiary concerns.

A. S.] Simone, what will you personally do in the coming French elections?

S. de B.] Me? I shan't be voting.

Paris, 1980

'Being a woman is not enough'

ALICE SCHWARZER] *La Cérémonie des Adieux* has just been published in German; Sartre's letters, which you are currently working on in France, will be published shortly. So let us talk about your relationship with Sartre: this relationship which was – and may still be – *the* model of a relationship based on love and freedom. It is now over two years since Sartre died. What new information will we glean from these two books, what new things about him and the two of you?

SIMONE DE BEAUVOIR] That it was a very tender and at the same time a very happy relationship. And a very trusting relationship, intellectually and emotionally. That comes over in the letters Sartre wrote to me when he was a prisoner-of-war (in very, very good conditions, he even had a desk). He had written a preface to *The Age of Reason* which he was very pleased with. But after I had criticised it, he tore it up and threw it away. In short, the letters show my critical influence on him, as well as his critical influence on me. Inspiration was a very personal matter for each of us, but when it came to putting words down on paper subsequently, each of us was extraordinarily receptive to the other person's criticisms. The letters also show the total trust he had in me where his emotional life was concerned, because he told me all about his affairs, right down to the details.

A. S.] Didn't that hurt?

S. de B.] No. We had complete and utter trust in one another. Each of us knew that the other one was the most important person in our lives – whatever happened.

A. S.] And you never had any doubts?

S. de B.] Once. I described it in my memoirs. I had one moment of hesitation because I did not know the other woman ... It was Dolores, whom I call M. in my memoirs, in America in 1944–45. It was just after the war, when everybody was letting their hair down. He spoke of her in terms of such friendship and respect that for a moment I thought: Maybe she is closer to him than I am? I put the question to him and his response was: You are the person I am with!

A. S.] And this special place was never called into question either by him or by you?

S. de B.] No, never. Perhaps because Sartre was very proud, and quite certain that no other man would ever be a serious rival to him ...

A. S.] On reading *La Cérémonie des Adieux*, one realises the sexual act was never very important to Sartre. I assume therefore that your relationship was never strongly based on sexuality simply because of that. Was that an advantage? Did it at least exclude physical jealousy? And diminish the pain of readjustment once the sexual attraction receded?

S. de B.] Perhaps ... But I should add that there was no intellectual jealousy either; we were both far too self-confident to fear that another person could become more important. In fact, the sex act in the strict sense did not interest Sartre particularly, he liked touching. In the first two or three years, sexual relations with Sartre were very important to me because I discovered sexuality with him. Later, it declined in importance between us, simply because it didn't mean so much to Sartre either. We maintained a sexual relationship for another fifteen or twenty years. But it wasn't the most important thing.

A. S.] The essential thing between you was your intellectual relationship, I think. What is your reaction to the widely held view of you as 'la grande Sartreuse', 'Sartre's star pupil'?

s. de b.] I think it is completely and utterly wrong! Of course, in philosophical terms, he was creative and I am not − but there are any number of men who are not creative either. I always recognised his superiority in that area. So where Sartre's philosophy is concerned, it is fair to say that I took my cue from him, because I also embraced existentialism for myself. There were, however, many things we discussed and even worked on together. For example, while he was working on *Being and Nothingness*, I opposed some of his ideas. And sometimes he changed things a bit.

a. s.] For example?

s. de b.] Well, in the first version of *Being and Nothingness*, he talked of freedom as though it were quasi-total for everybody − or at least as though it were always possible to exercise one's freedom. But I insisted on the fact that there are situations where freedom cannot be exercised, or where it is simply a mystification. He accepted that. Later he ascribed great significance to the situation a person finds himself in.

a. s.] That was in 1941–42 − before you both embraced Marxism . . . ?

s. de b.] Yes.

a. s.] And what were you doing at the time?

s. de b.] I was independent of Sartre, because I was writing my own books, my own novels. I had opted for literature. Even *The Second Sex* with its philosophical background of Sartrean existentialism was still exclusively the creation of *my* vision of women. That was how *I* had experienced it.

a. s.] What is your explanation of the fact that, even

with someone like Sartre, who was very attractive, both as a person, and intellectually, you did not fall into the trap of wanting to be 'his wife'? That you did not decline into a relative being, the 'woman at his side'? What seems to you to have been the decisive factor in your life explaining the fact that you have succeeded in leading an autonomous existence?

s. de b.] The formative influences in my early years. The fact that I always wanted my own career! That I always wanted to write, long before I met Sartre! That I had dreams, not fantasies, but very bold dreams, things I knew I wanted to do, long before I met Sartre! To be happy, I owed it to myself to fulfil my life. And to me fulfilment meant work, first and foremost.

a. s.] And what was Sartre's attitude?

s. de b.] He was my main source of encouragement. After my doctorate, I had worked very hard, and I wanted to relax a bit, to sink back into happiness, into Sartre's love . . . And he was the person who said, 'But Castor, why have you stopped thinking, why aren't you working? I thought you wanted to write? You don't want to become a housewife, do you . . . ?' He was very insistent that I should maintain my own autonomy, especially by writing.

a. s.] If Sartre had not met you, he probably would have ended up in a classic married relationship . . .

s. de b.] Sartre married? He would have hated every minute of it! But it is true that it would have been very easy to drive him into a corner. That guilty conscience of his . . . But then he used to get over it pretty quickly too.

a. s.] A guilty conscience, or feelings of guilt, are very common among women. Is that a feeling you have experienced?

S. de B.] No, I never had a guilty conscience in that sense. A few pangs sometimes, when I brought a friendship to a close in a brutal manner. I was not always very proud of that. But all in all, I've always had a clear conscience – sometimes that was almost unconscious, I think.

A. S.] I think that, in general, you are the kind of person who doesn't particularly enjoy delving into herself too much . . .

S. de B.] That's true. I don't apply my analyses to myself all that often. It is not in my nature.

A. S.] Jean Genet once said of the two of you that you were the man and Sartre was the woman in your relationship. What did he mean exactly?

S. de B.] He was trying to say that, in his view, Sartre was a great deal more sensitive than me, sensitive in a way that could be described as 'feminine'. My behaviour, on the other hand, was much more brusque. But that had a lot to do with Genet's relationship with women, whom he doesn't exactly like very much . . .

A. S.] But there is a grain of truth in it. You can be as stubborn as a mule – you say so yourself. You have a lot of energy, intellectually you can be very penetrating, not to say downright frosty if you are faced with people or situations you do not like . . . You are a very all-or-nothing person.

S. de B.] That's true.

A. S.] I know quite a few women who have been made to pay, so to speak, for insisting on the right to show their intelligence and strength of character. People around them make them feel: so you are 'as good as any man', are you? Well, then you are not desirable 'as a woman'! Have you come up against that?

S. de B.] No.

A. S.] So you have never been tempted to play the 'little woman' so as to compensate for your 'masculine' traits?

S. de B.] Oh no, never. I was working and I had Sartre. And things happened of their own accord. I did not chase after them . . . and so when I fell in love with Nelson Algren in America – in a foreign country, with his charms and all the qualities he had – I didn't have to put on an act or behave out of character! He was in love with me too.

A. S.] Was your erotic desire always bound up with your emotions?

S. de B.] I think so, yes. In fact, I never desired any man unless he desired me too. It was always the other person's desire for me that swept me away.

A. S.] Very cautious . . .

S. de B.] Yes. Perhaps, occasionally, I had different fantasies . . . But in real life, there was no man with any power to move me, unless there was already a deep bond of friendship between us.

A. S.] No sudden rush of physical desire? No one-night stands, where anyone would do, no matter who?

S. de B.] Oh no, never! That is quite, quite alien to me. It may be puritanical, it may be the result of my upbringing. But whatever, it never, never happened. Not even when I had no relationship on the go and therefore had no sex life for a while. All the same, I would never have ever thought of just going out and getting myself a man . . .

A. S.] Is this reserve 'feminine'?

S. de B.] I don't know.

A. S.] When you talk about your own sexuality, you only ever talk about men. Have you never had a sexual relationship with a woman?

S. de B.] No. I have had some very important friend-

ships with women, of course, some very close relationships, sometimes close in a physical sense. But they never
aroused erotic passion on my part.

A. S.] Why not?

s. de B.] It is most probably the way my upbringing has
conditioned me. I mean my entire education, not just
what I was taught at home, but all the reading and all the
influences which shaped me as a child and which pushed
me in the direction of heterosexuality.

A. S.] Do you mean that you accept homosexuality on a
theoretical level, for yourself as well?

s. de B.] Yes, completely and utterly. Women should
not let themselves be conditioned exclusively to male
desire any more. And in any case, I think that these days
every woman is a bit . . . a bit homosexual. Quite simply,
because women are more desirable than men.

A. S.] How so?

s. de B.] Because they are more attractive, softer, their
skin is nicer. And generally they have more charm. It is
quite often the case with the usual married couple that
the woman is nicer, more lively, more attractive, more
amusing, even on an intellectual level.

A. S.] One might say that what you are saying is a bit
sexist . . .

s. de B.] No. But, of course, it is a result of the different
conditioning, and the reality, of the sexes. These days
men often have these slightly ridiculous traits which
Sartre used to complain about too. They love to theorise
in such a self-important way, they are so inflexible, so
lacking in liveliness.

A. S.] True. But women have their faults too. And the
new thing is that they are even proud of them. In
Germany, for example, but not only there, we are facing

a renaissance of 'femininity', which has been called the 'new femininity', but is in actual fact as old as the hills; the emphasis on feelings in place of intellect, a 'natural' pacific character instead of a willingness to fight, the mystification of motherhood presented as a creative act in itself, etc. Before the women's movement began, you formulated the creed of the new feminism: in *The Second Sex* you wrote, 'One is not born, but rather becomes, a woman.' What is your reaction to the return of some women to the idea of a 'woman's nature'?

s. de b.] I think it's a return to the enslavement of women, pure and simple! After all, motherhood is still the most skilful way there is of turning women into slaves. I don't mean that every women who is a mother is automatically a slave – there can be modes of existence where motherhood does not mean slavery. But these days it still comes down to much the same thing. Yet as long as people think that a woman's main task is to have children, women will not concern themselves with politics and technology, and furthermore, they will not dispute men's superiority. This new interpretation of 'motherhood' and 'femininity' is really an attempt to relegate women to the level they were at before.

a. s.] And it is very convenient at a time of international economic recession.

s. de b.] Exactly. Given that one can hardly tell women that washing up saucepans is their divine mission, they are told that bringing up children is their divine mission. But the way things are in this world, bringing up children has a great deal in common with washing up saucepans. In this way, women are thrust back into the role of a relative being, a second-class person.

a. s.] Has feminism failed in some way, then?

s. de b.] I think that actually feminism has only really got through to a very small number of women so far. Certain campaigns have reached large numbers of women; for example, the struggle for the right to an abortion. But now that feminism seems to represent a threat to a lot of people – because of unemployment and because male privileges are under attack – there is a reaction against it: the stereotype, which remains deep-seated in the majority of women, is being brought to the fore. Most women have in fact remained the 'little woman' at heart . . . Femininity has re-acquired a certain ideological value and attempts are being made to resurrect the image of the 'ordinary woman' – which feminism has torn to shreds – secondary, modest and so on. Tears are shed for this image of woman, which feminism tore to shreds, and attempts are being made to revive it.

a. s.] Some questions for you as an existentialist and a Marxist. What is the score for women's freedom under current conditions? Where do you see scope for action nowadays? And where are the limits that we will inevitably come up against? What route can women take, what strategy can they employ to break out of this vicious circle of 'femininity'? And have we feminists so far followed the right path?

s. de b.] Hard to say. It is already good that something has been done. And the circumstances are anything but favourable . . . But it's true that from very early on there have been things in this movement which have not been so good. For instance, some women's insistence on repudiating absolutely everything that comes from men. They won't do anything the man's way: whether it be organisation, career, creative work or concrete action.

I've always thought that one should simply borrow and make use of the systems men have at their disposal. I know that feminists are very divided about the path to follow. Should women take on more and more jobs and join in the rat race with men? If they do so, they will certainly take on some of men's qualities as well as some of their shortcomings. Or, by contrast, should women completely abstain from all of that? In the first case, they would gain more power; in the second they would relegate themselves to powerlessness. Of course, if women simply gain power in order to use it in the same way as men do anyway ... Well, that's no way to transform society. In my view, the real task of feminism can only be the transformation of society along with the transformation of women's place in it.

A. S.] You have chosen the first path; you have written and created 'as a man'. And at the same time, you have attempted to change the world.

S. de B.] Yes. And I believe that a two-pronged strategy of this kind is the only way. We mustn't refuse to take on qualities that are termed masculine! We must be ready to take the risk of involving ourselves in this male world which is, quite simply, the world itself to a large degree. Of course, this way a woman runs the risk of betraying other women, and of betraying feminism. She will think she has escaped . . . But the other way, she runs the risk of suffocating in 'femininity'.

A. S.] One way or another, women have known rejection and humiliation.

S. de B.] My particular piece of good fortune is that I have never been humiliated. I haven't suffered from the fact of being a woman. Even though – as I said in the Preface to *The Second Sex* – it annoys me greatly when people say things like, 'You think so and so because you are a woman.' I have always replied, 'That's really ridiculous – do you think so and so because you are a man?'

A. S.] On the subject of literature – the same debate going on among feminists: should one encourage quality or quantity? In other words, should one evaluate and criticise women as severely as men? Or should one just be glad that women are writing at all?

S. de B.] I think one must be able to say, 'No: no, that won't do! Write something else, try and do better. Set higher standards for yourselves! Being a woman is not enough.' I receive many manuscripts from women who hope to be published. They are housewives, forty or fifty years old, without jobs, the children have left home and they have time on their hands. A lot of women turn to writing then. Mostly their life story, almost always an unhappy childhood. And they think it is interesting . . . Writing things down can be important for one's state of mind, but that doesn't mean it has to be published. No, I think women must be very demanding with themselves.

A. S.] Has the existence of the new women's movement had any direct effects on you?

S. de B.] It has made me more sensitive to details, to this everyday sexism, which hardly registers otherwise, because it seems so 'normal'. For some years now, a group of feminists in Paris have been editing texts for *Les Temps Modernes*, pointing out the way they express 'everyday sexism', which I myself had never been really aware of before.

A. S.] Before the women's movement existed, you used to say 'they' when you talked about women. Now you say 'we'.

s. de b.] 'We' meaning 'we feminists', not 'we women'.

a. s.] Nowadays, though, everyone is climbing on the 'feminism' bandwagon. For example, the growing West German peace movement includes women under the feminist banner, such as 'Mothers who want to save tomorrow's world for their children', 'Women, the bearers of life', and even 'Women are more peaceable than men by nature' – that is, men are allegedly 'destructive' by nature.

s. de b.] That is absurd! Absurd, because women must fight for peace as human beings, not as women. This type of argument is completely senseless; after all, if women are mothers, men are fathers. Anyway, so far, if anything, women have clung too much to their child-bearing abilities, their 'maternal instinct', which amounts to a relapse into the myth of a woman's role. That shouldn't be a first priority. Like men, women can fight so that future generations will not have to lay down their lives. But that has very little to do with the fact of being a mother or a woman oneself. In short, women should drop this 'feminine' argument once and for all, despite and because of the fact that people are encouraging them to fight for peace in the name of their femininity or their maternal instinct. It's simply a male trick to reduce women to their wombs. And in any case, women who come to power behave no differently from men. You can see that in the case of Indira Gandhi, Golda Meir, Mrs Thatcher and others. They certainly don't suddenly become angels of mercy or of peace.

a. s.] After the Second World War, you and Sartre became militant intellectuals. For many years your involvement in politics was both passionate and active; you both wrote and you both took direct action in order to bring more justice and freedom to the world. You placed some hope in the revolutions in the Soviet Union, China and Cuba – and you had to accept disappointment. The crimes committed by the French during the Algerian war upset you personally. You relate that in your memoirs. You fought openly, and courageously, for decolonisation, and wept for nights on end, 'ashamed of being French'. What now? What is your view of current political developments in the world in general, and in France in particular? Did you vote for Mitterand?

s. de b.] Yes, because it meant a little more justice as a result. Higher taxes for people with a lot of money and better pensions for the poor. And there has been some progress on the feminist level. Yvette Roudy* is a Minister with her own budget, after all. She has been giving women, and indeed feminists, quite a lot of money to found research centres and magazines. She has started a campaign for contraception and abortion on demand. In fact, in future, there is even a possibility that the Health Service will be paying for abortions. But otherwise . . . Quite honestly, I wasn't expecting any miracles. Nobody can work miracles, least of all in this difficult economic climate . . . This socialist government must tread with a very measured and cautious step. It has no option, otherwise it would be staring a revolution in the face. And there can be no question of that at the moment. Personally, I am against a violent, a bloody revolution, at the present time at least. The price would be too high. So, unfortunately, a complete transformation of the world order is not one of the items for discussion on the agenda. In my view, in current

* The Minister in the newly-established Women's Ministry.

conditions in France, it can only be a question of some slight improvement in society as it currently exists.

A. S.] In this conversation we have talked so much about men that I should like to conclude by mentioning the woman who has shared your life for more than ten years and who, since Sartre's death, is now probably the person dearest to you: Sylvie le Bon, thirty-nine years old, a teacher of philosophy. Such great friendships are uncommon between women.

S. de B.] I am not so sure. Many friendships between women endure, whereas love fades . . . Real friendships between men are very, very uncommon, I think. Largely because women say so much more to one another.

Paris, 1982